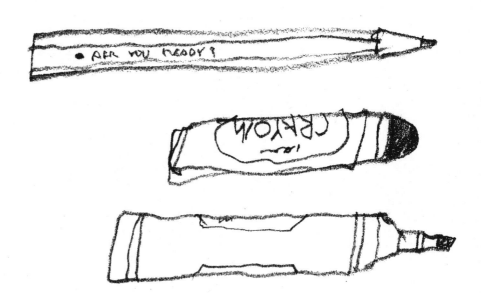

This Chronicle Books edition published in 2006.

Originally published in the United States in 2004 by Seuil/Chronicle under the ISBN 2-02-061396-4.

Originally published in Japan in 1990 by Bronze Publishing Inc. under the title *Rakugaki Ehon*.

Translation by Shoshanna Kirk-Jegousse.
Typeset in Avenir.

Manufactured in Singapore.

ISBN-13 978-0-8118-5509-9
ISBN-10 0-8118-5509-0

10 9 8 7 6 5 4 3

Chronicle Books LLC
680 Second Street, San Francisco, California 94107

www.chroniclekids.com

Scribbles

Really Giant

A^ Drawing and
Coloring Book

Taro Gomi

chronicle books · san francisco

This is a tree

Fill it with leaves

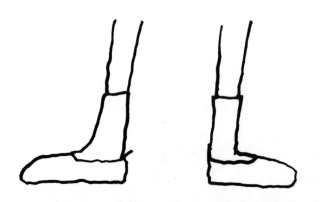

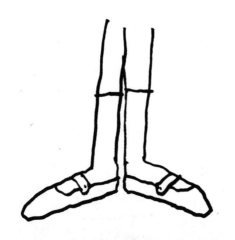

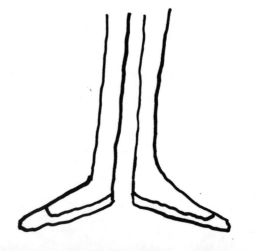

Can you draw them a bridge?

Draw some flowers

Draw butterflies, too

Draw the road

Color the circles

And try to stay within the lines

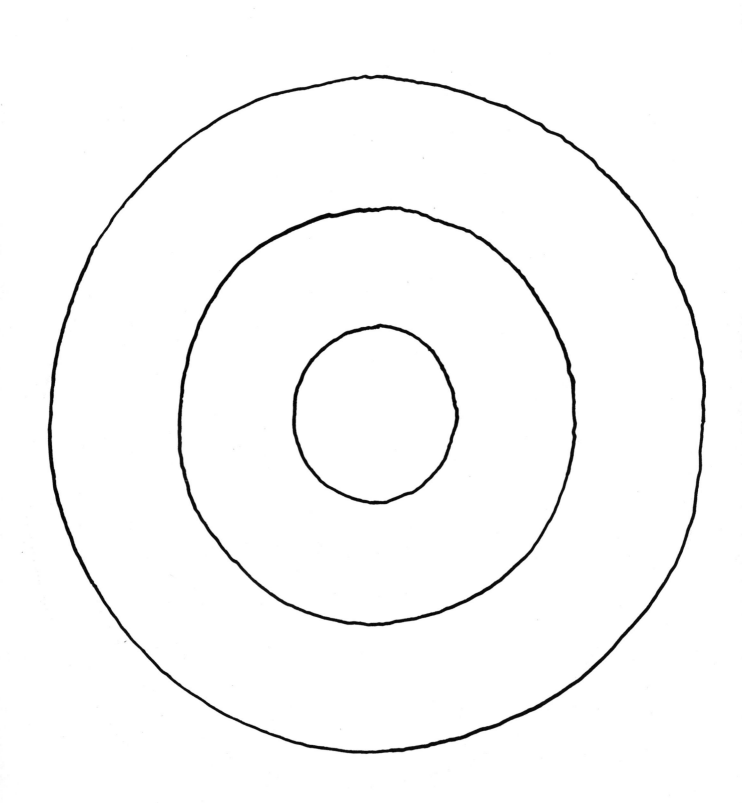

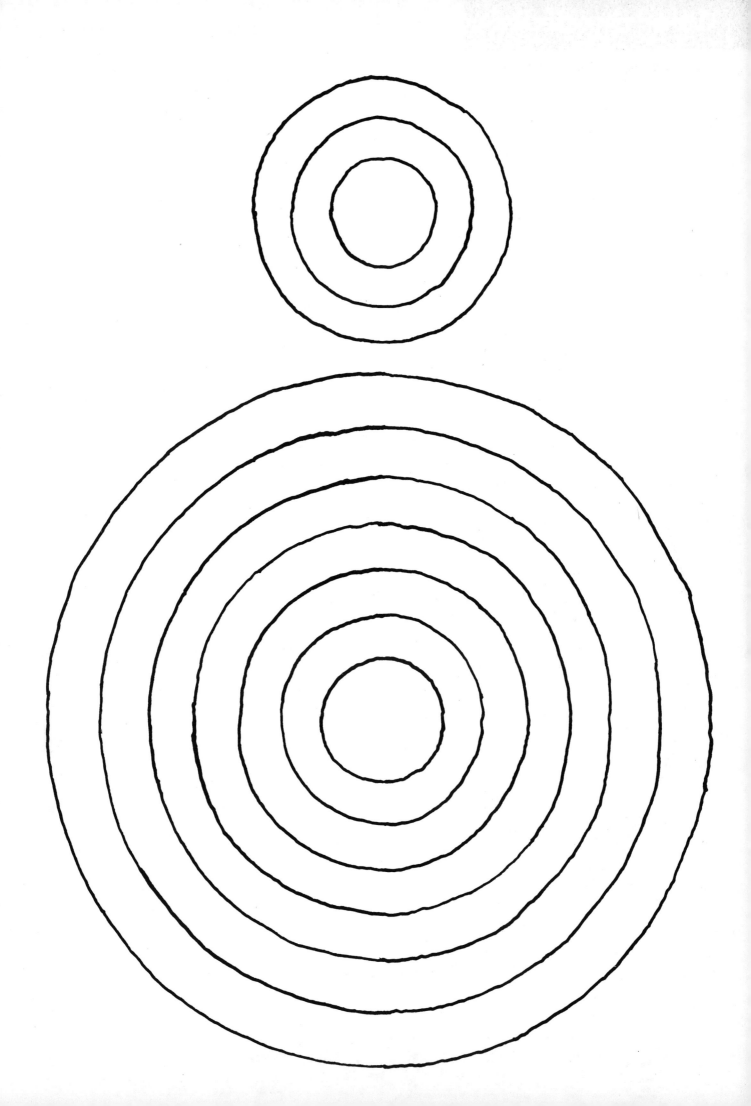

Who is looking out the windows?

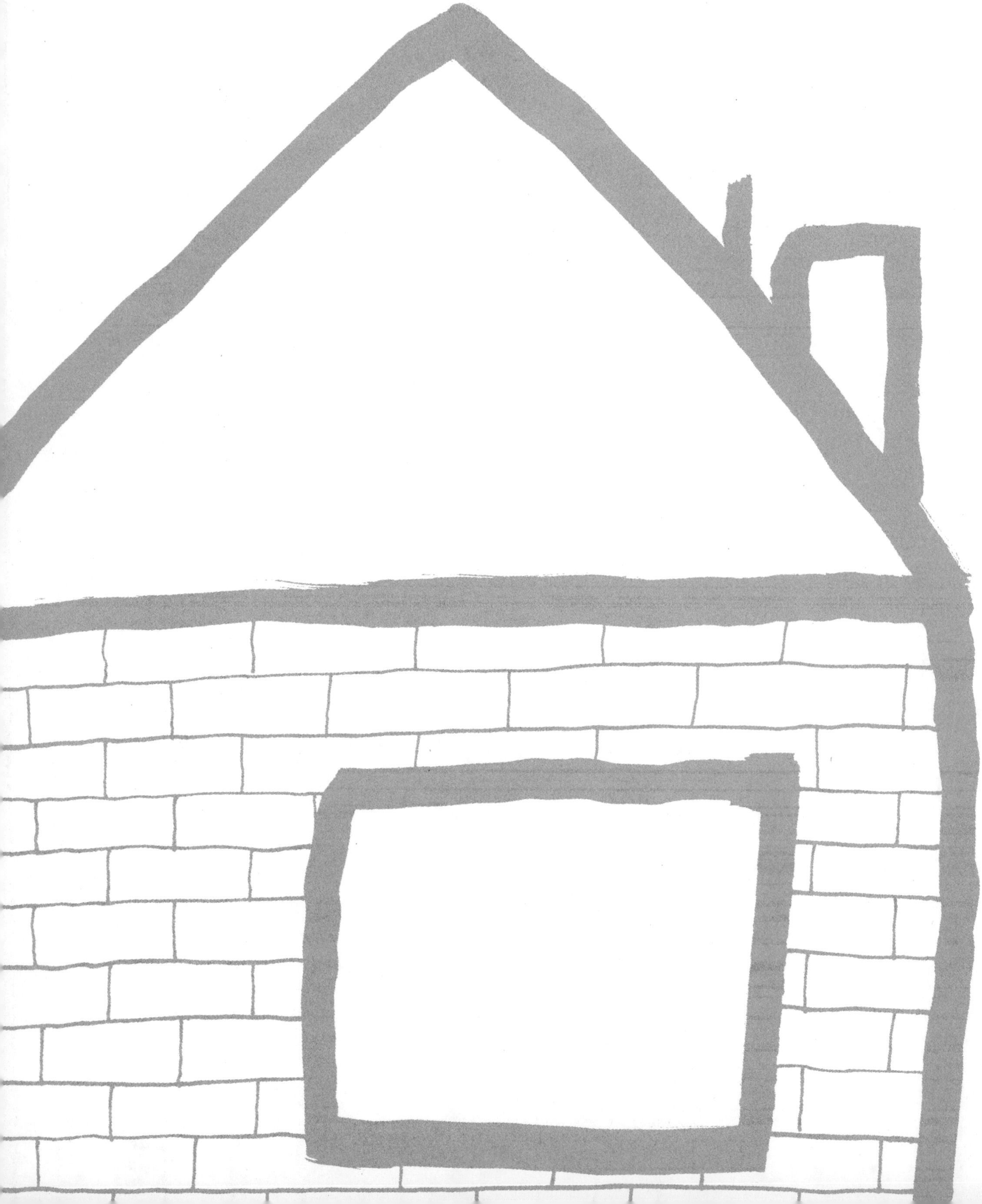

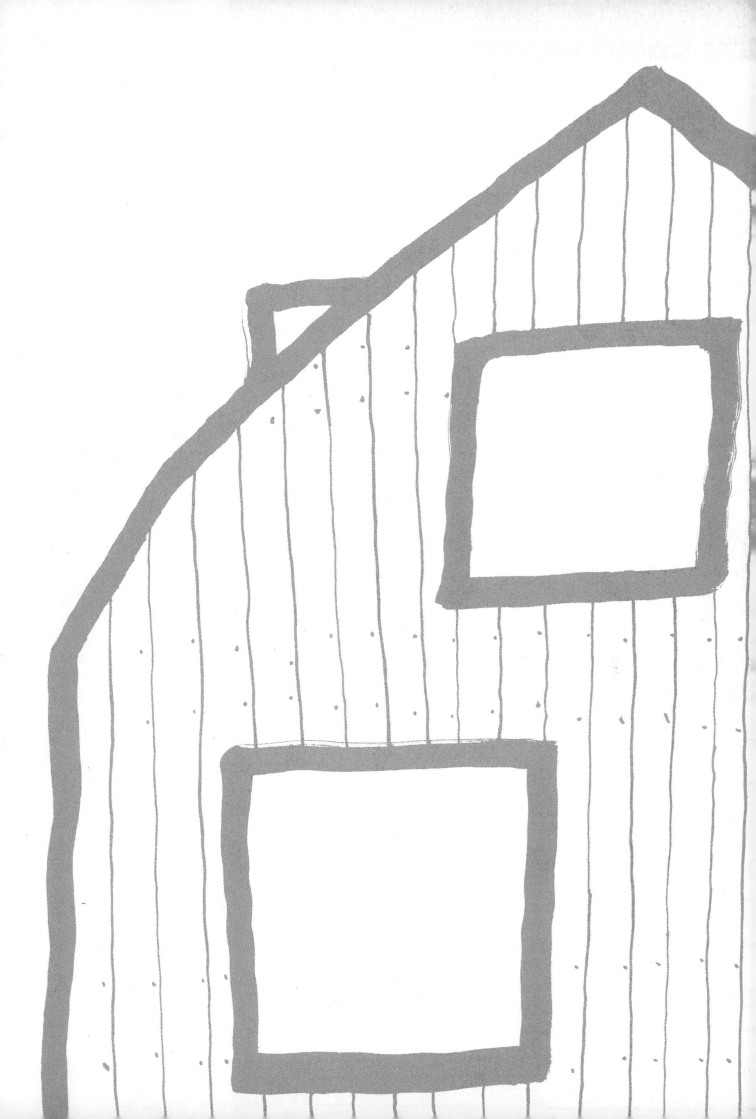

It's three o'clock

Draw the hands on the clock

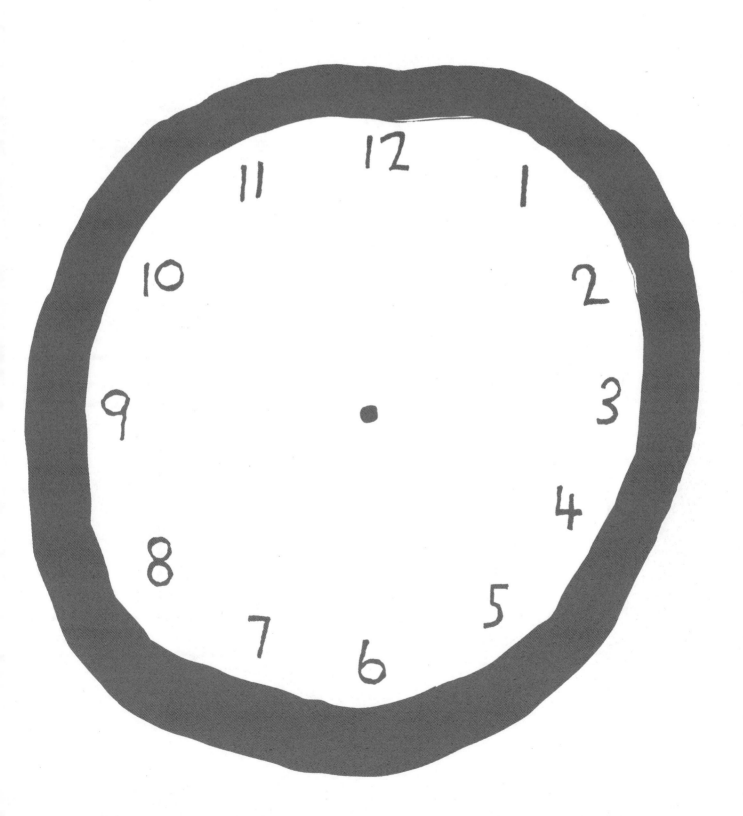

Now, it's eight-thirty

Draw something good to eat

Draw the rain pouring down

These are robots

They need arms and legs

Draw him a hat

Draw her a ribbon

It's a beautiful day today

Draw a bright sunny sky

Draw a dark cloudy sky

Draw lightening and rain

This is the sea

Draw some boats

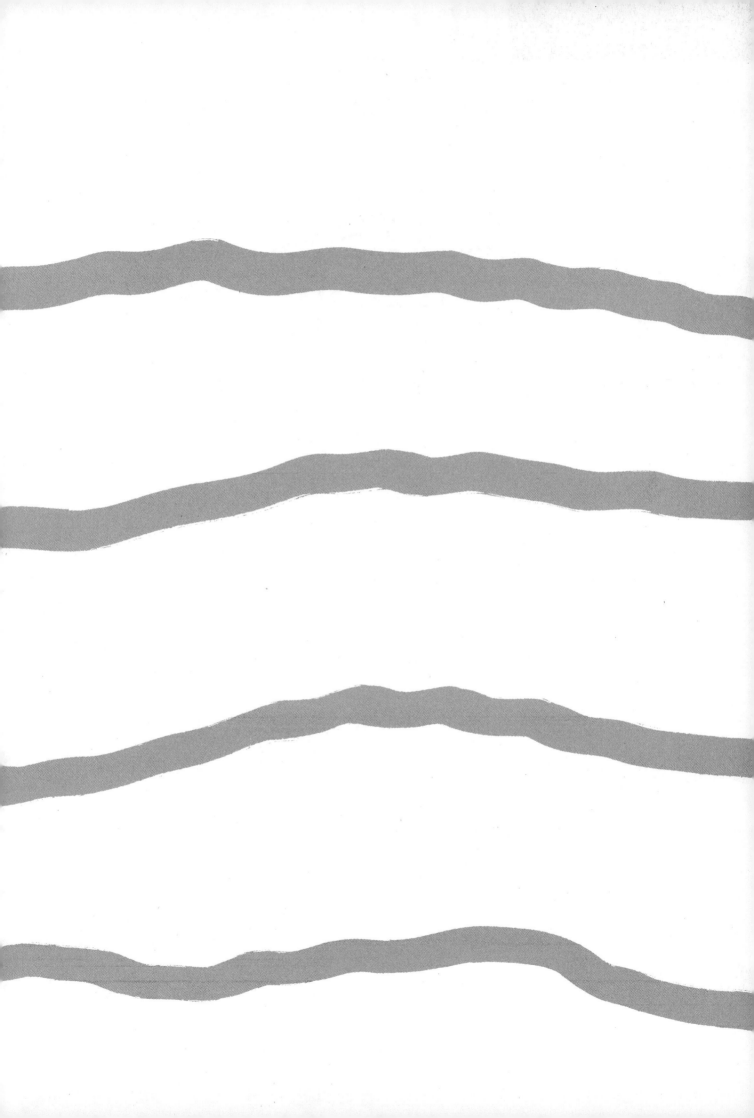

Make sure he doesn't eat the pigs!

It's snowing!

Draw a snake

Make it longer than this piece of rope

Draw a huge volcanic eruption

Draw exactly the same thing on the right-hand page

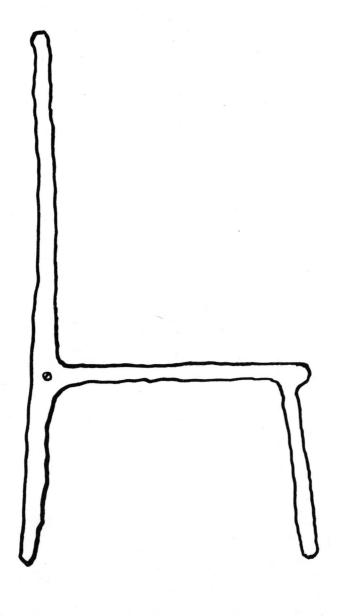

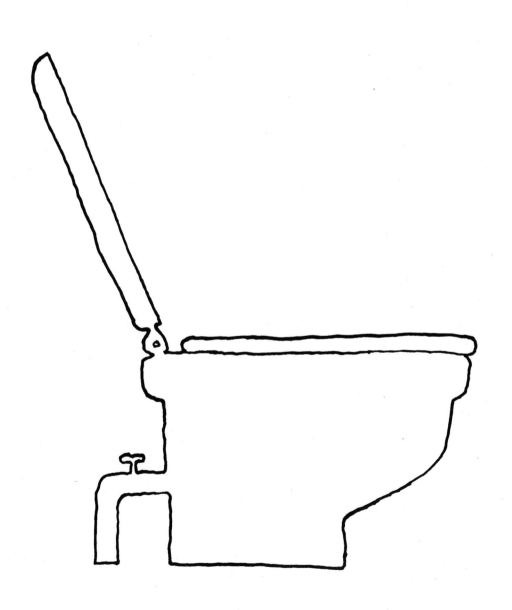

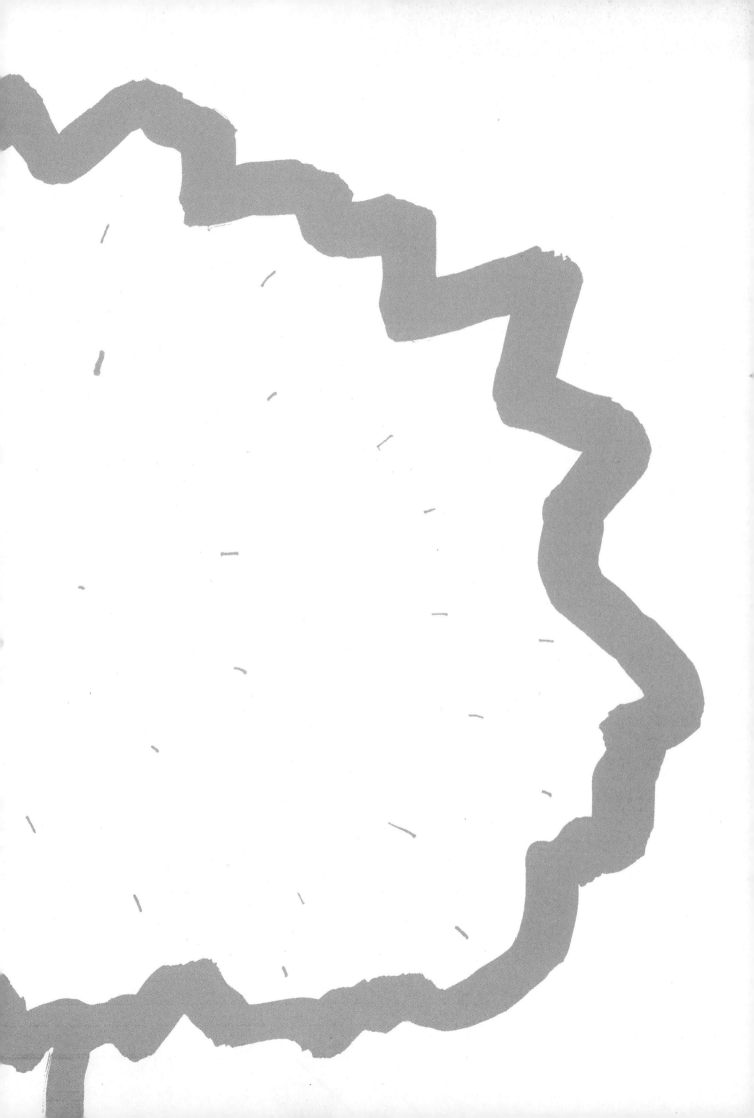

Draw houses in this landscape

Draw fields, schools and buildings, too

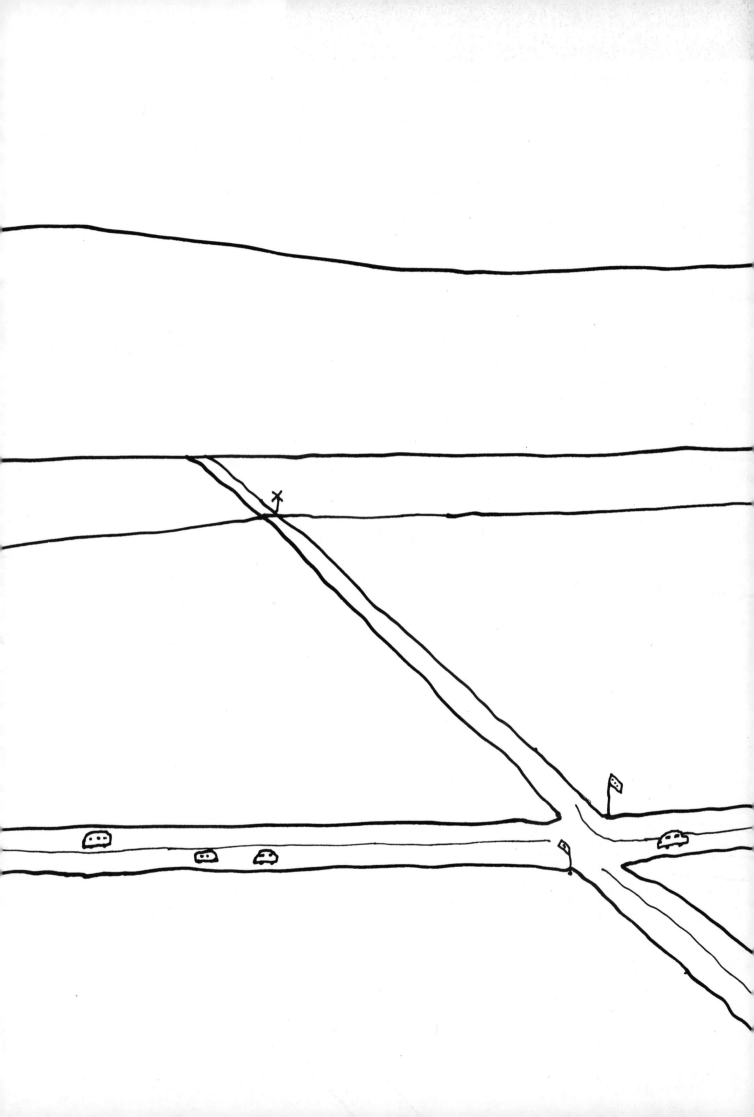

This is a mountain

Cover it with trees

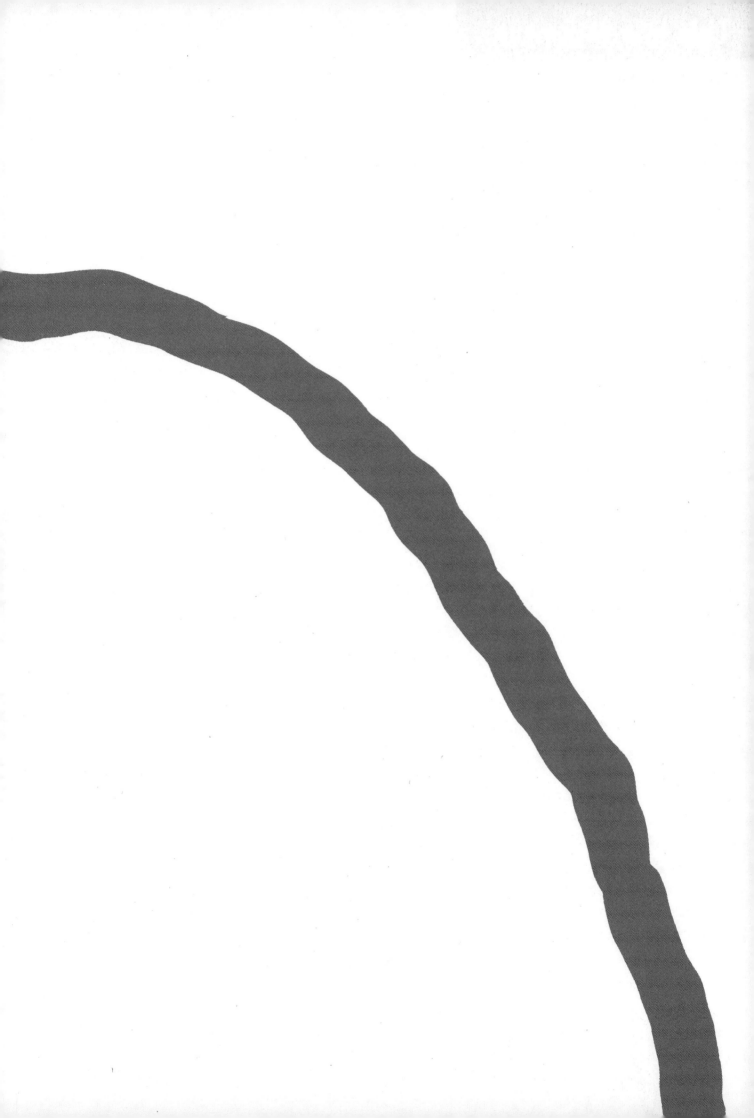

This is a staircase

Draw people walking up

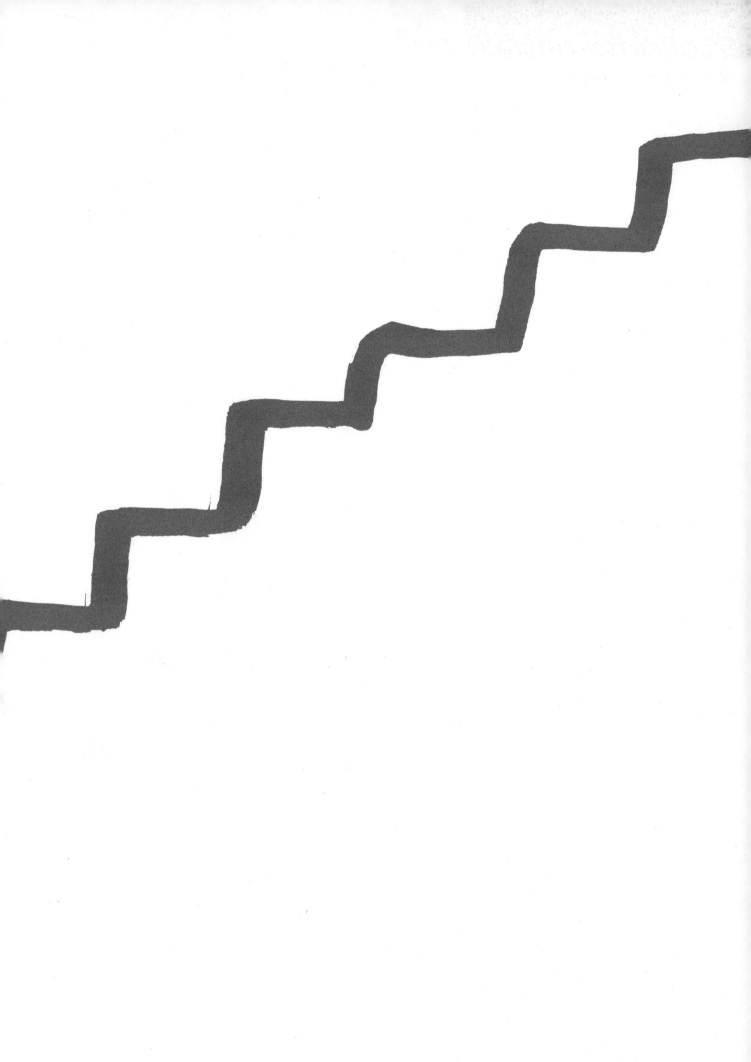

This is a staircase, too

Draw people walking down, and some people falling!

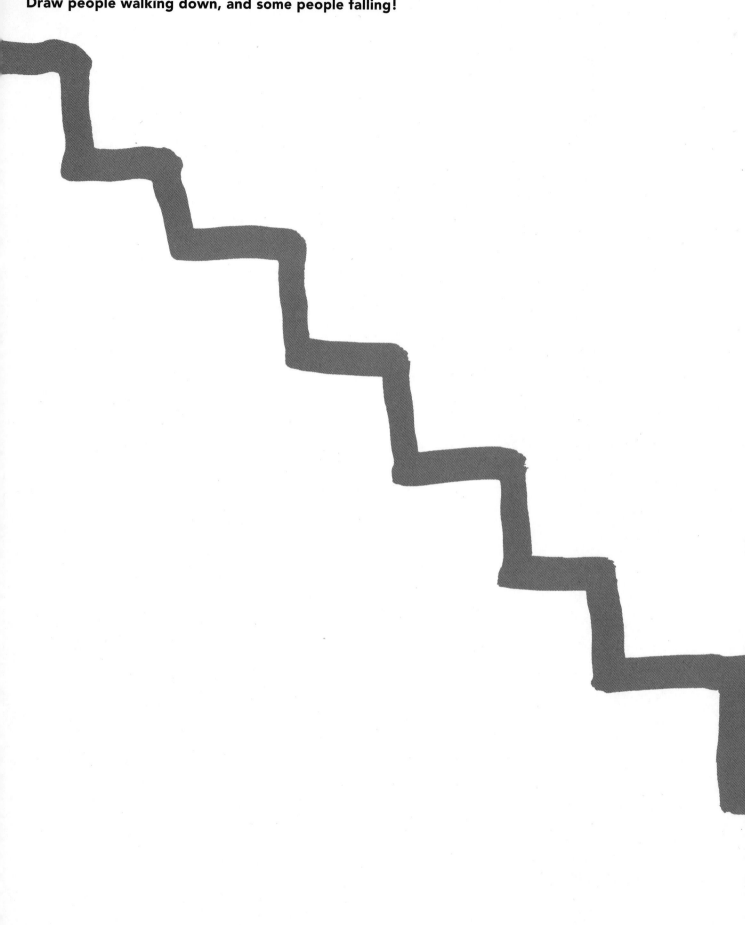

Draw a rainbow

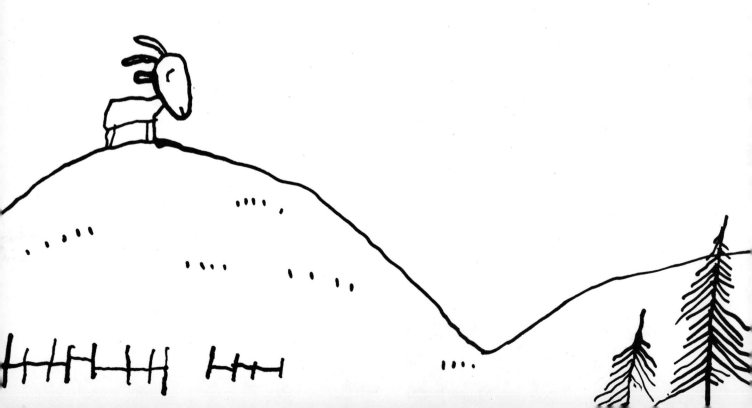

I am an octopus

Draw my tentacles

I am a squid

I need tentacles, too

Color these crayons

With crayons!

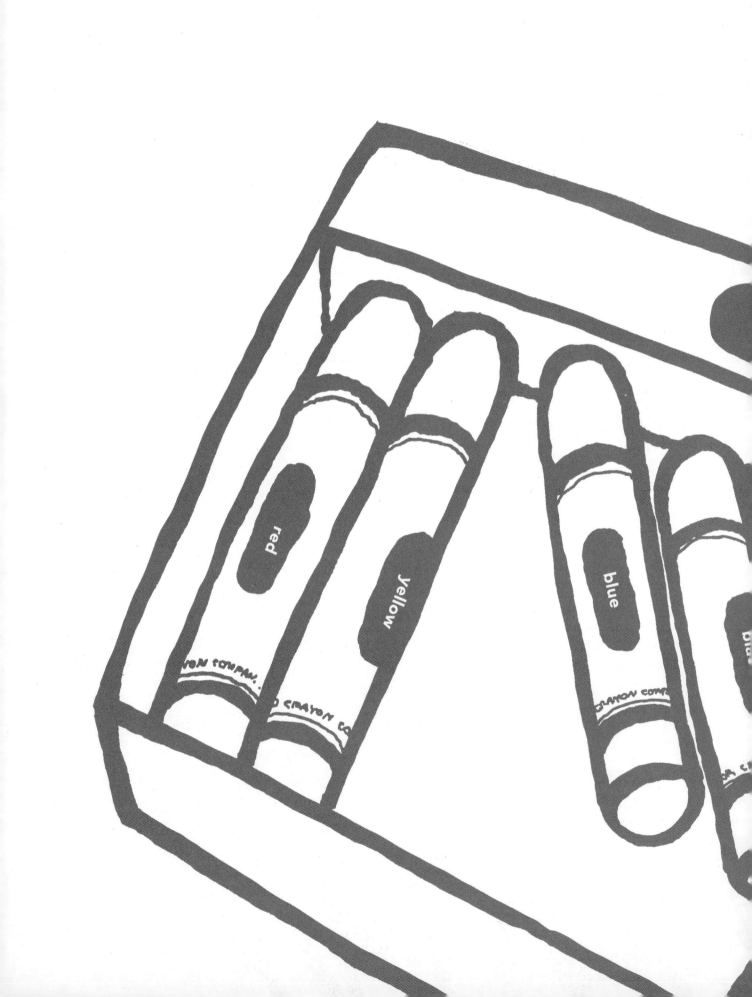

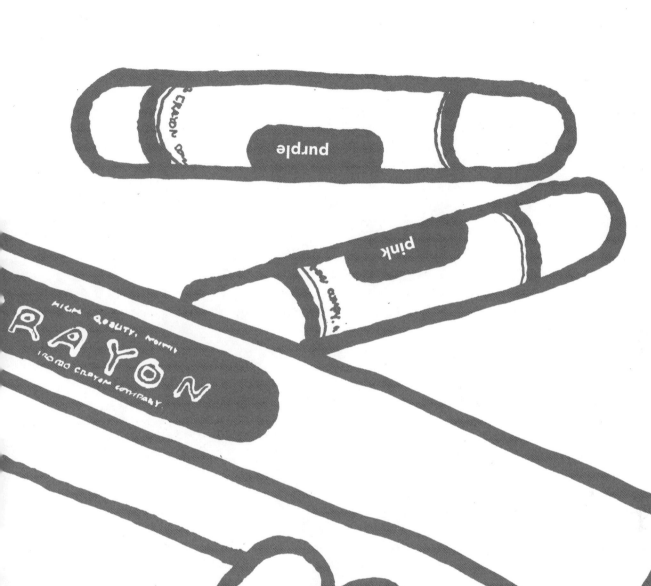

I'm five years old

Put five candles on my cake

This is a color game

Follow this code
★ red   ● yellow   ■ blue
▲ green   ◉ orange   ▣ purple

Don't use the wrong color!

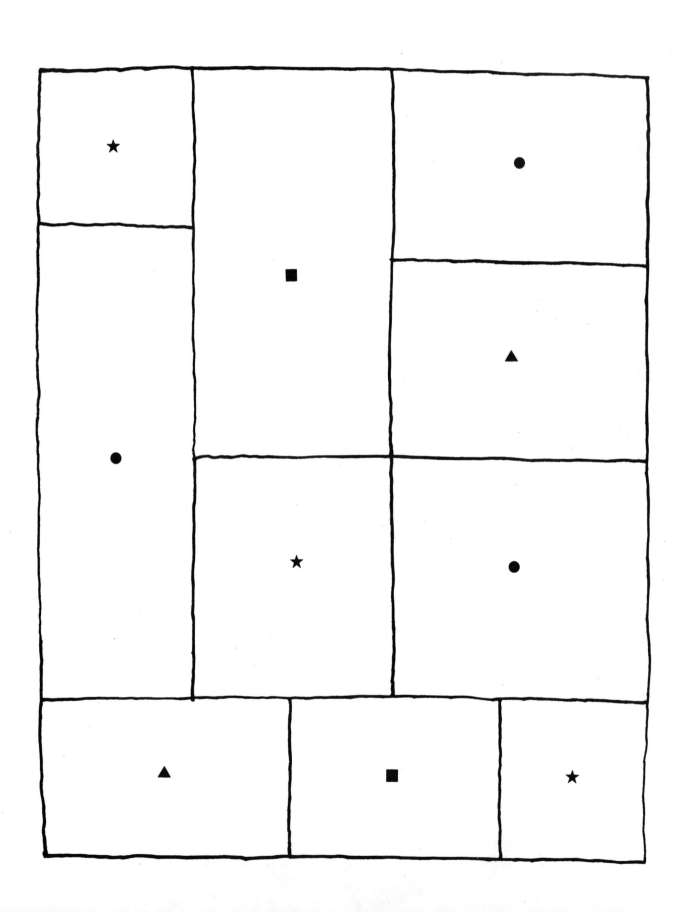

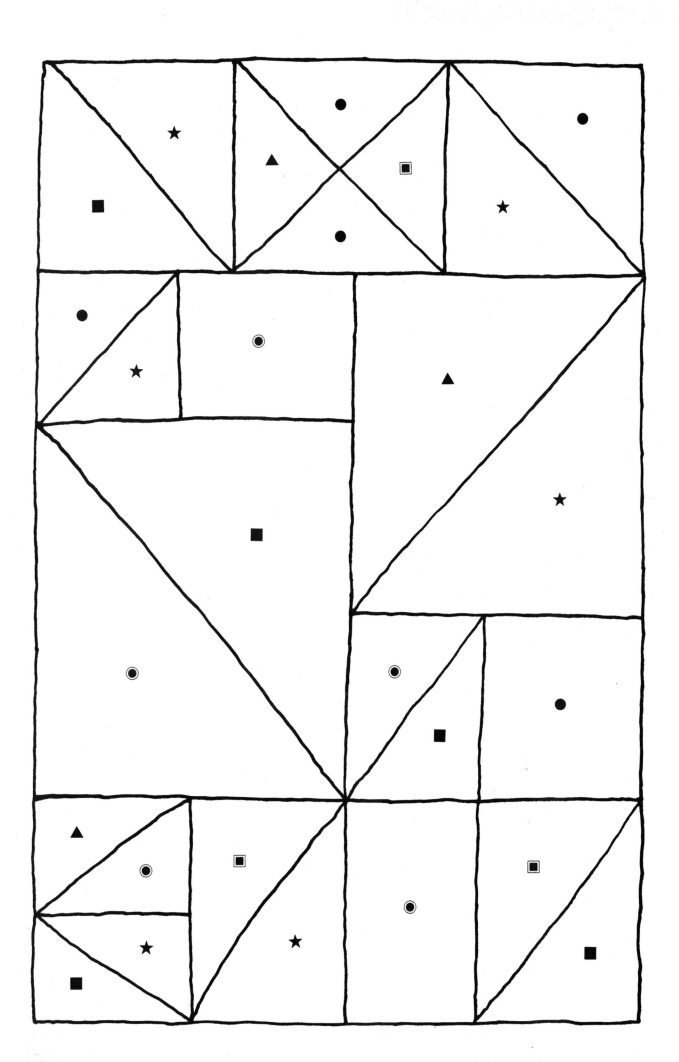

Draw some windows

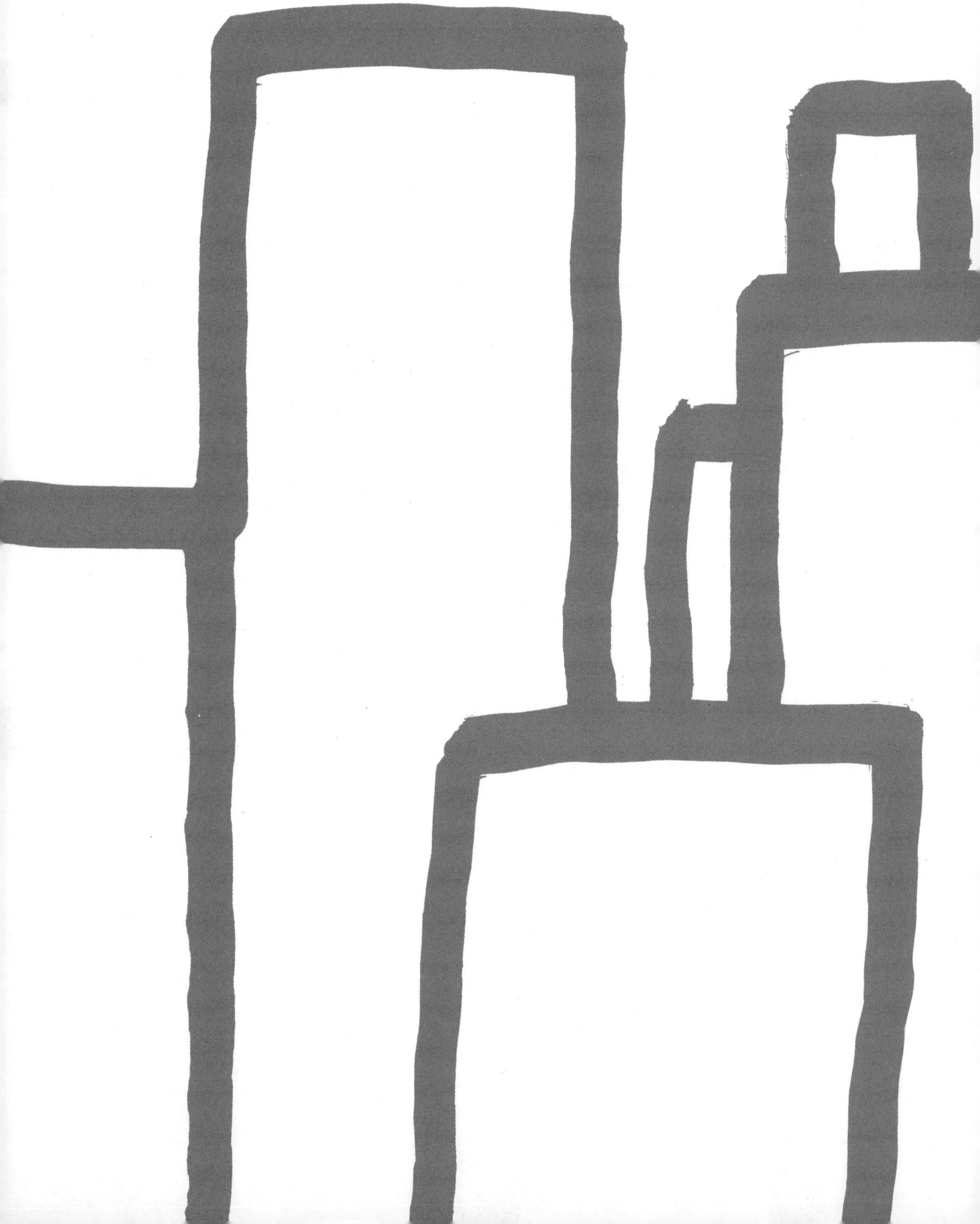

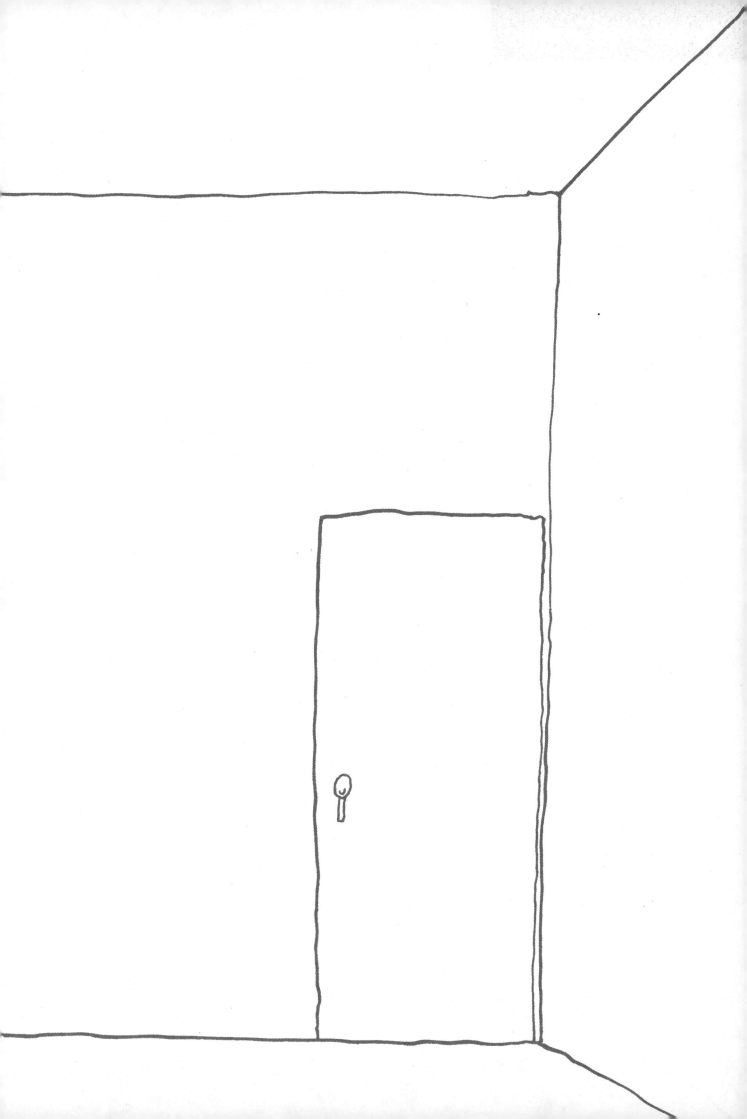

This horse needs legs

And a tail!

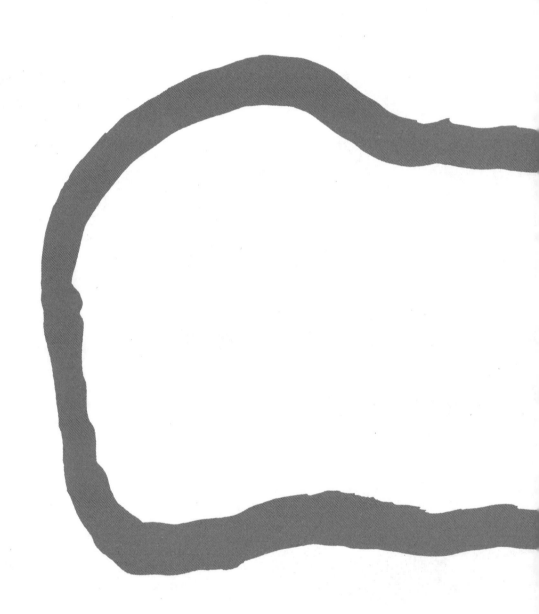

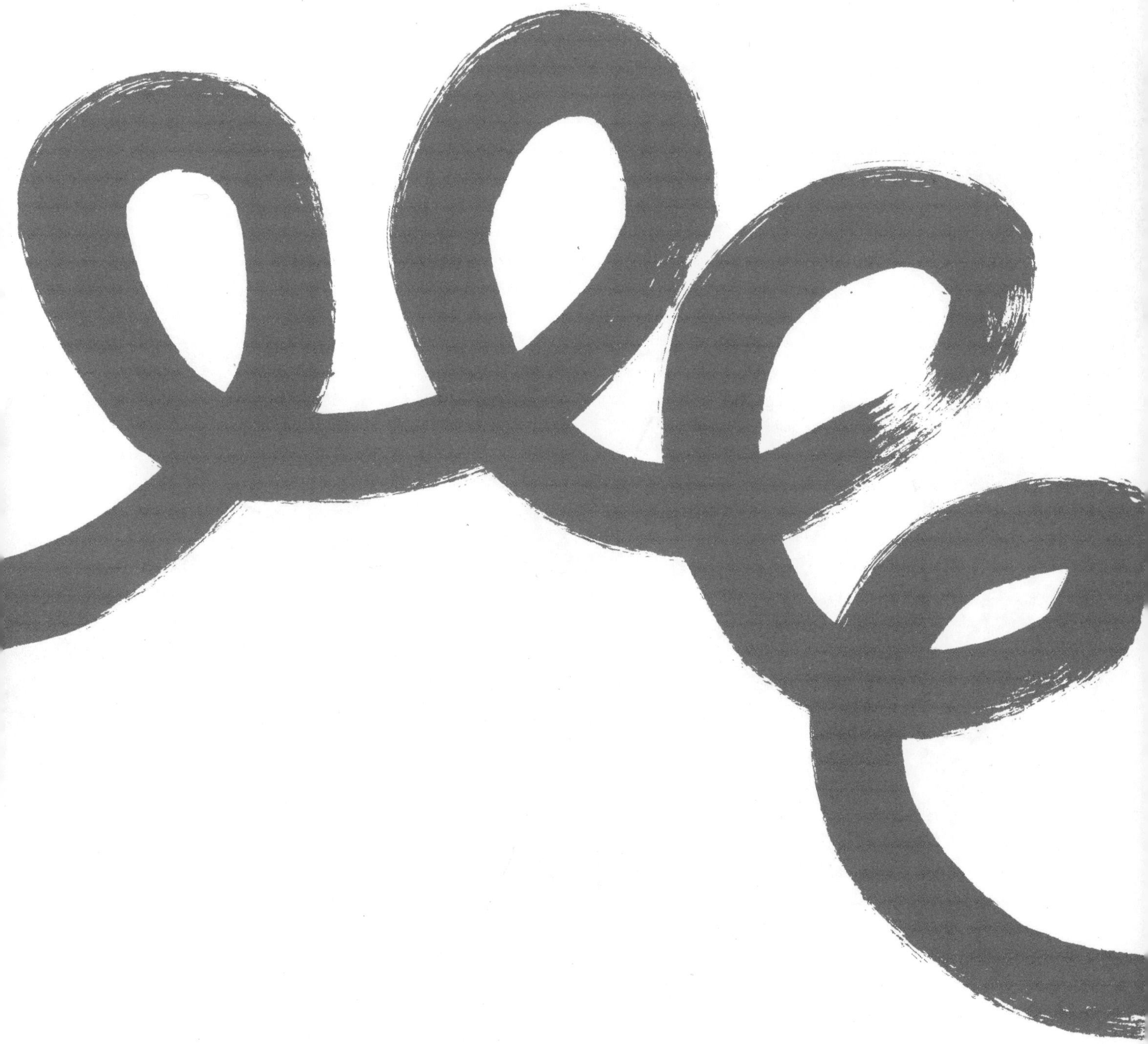

Draw something that spirals

Draw an angry face

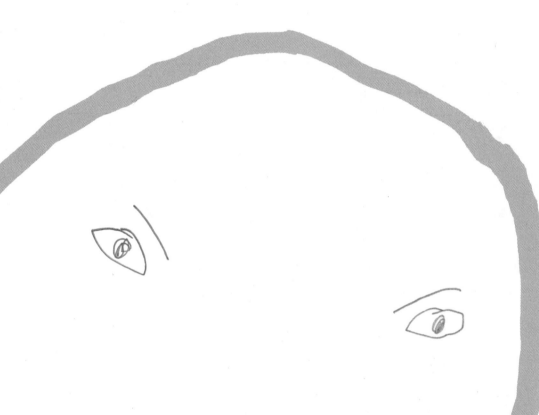

Color only the things you like

Make some rockets fly

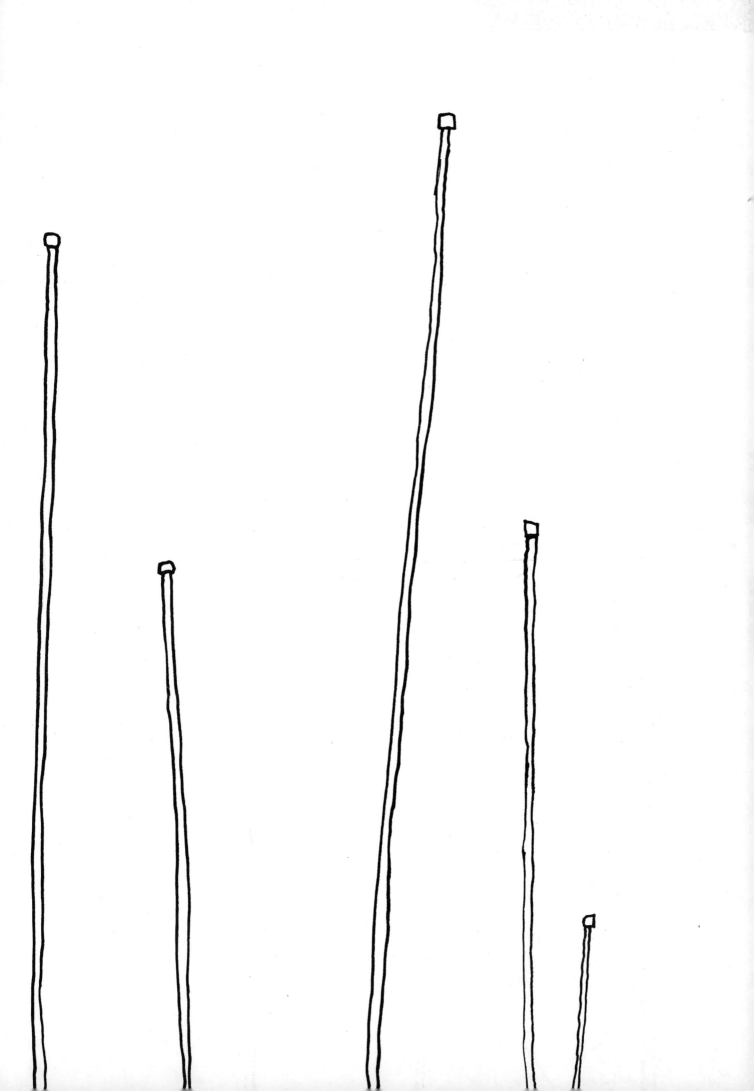

Draw their faces

Make the woman as friendly and the man as scary as you can

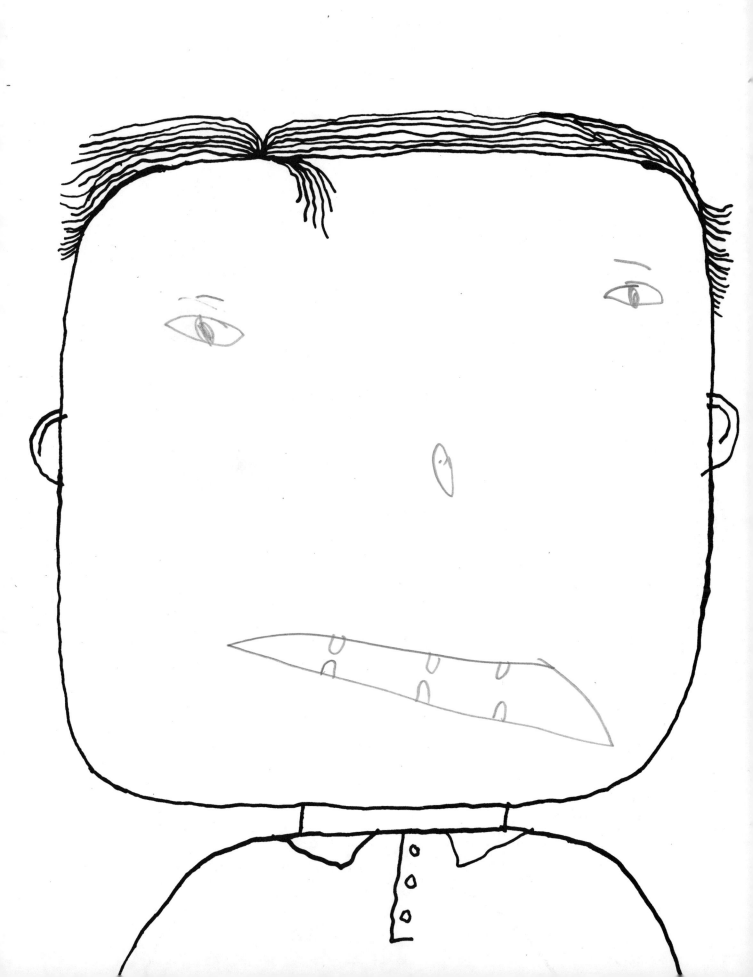

Draw some things that are round

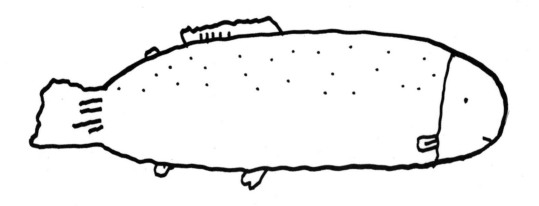

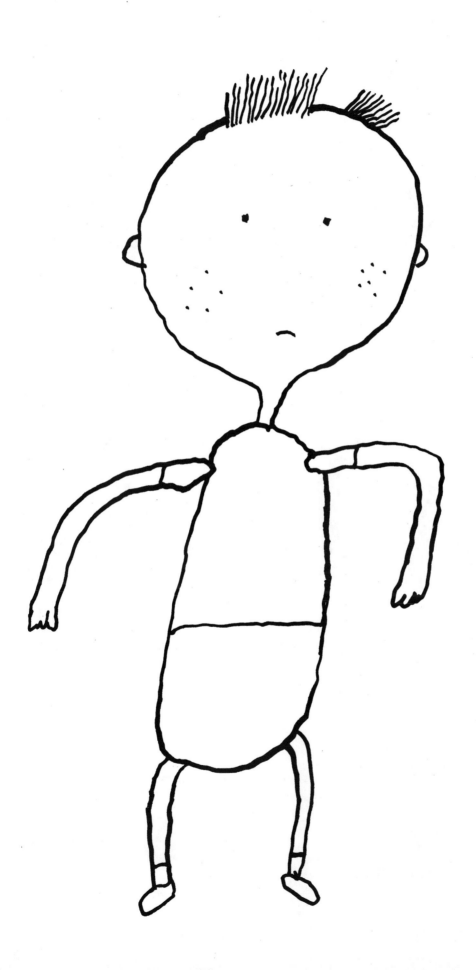

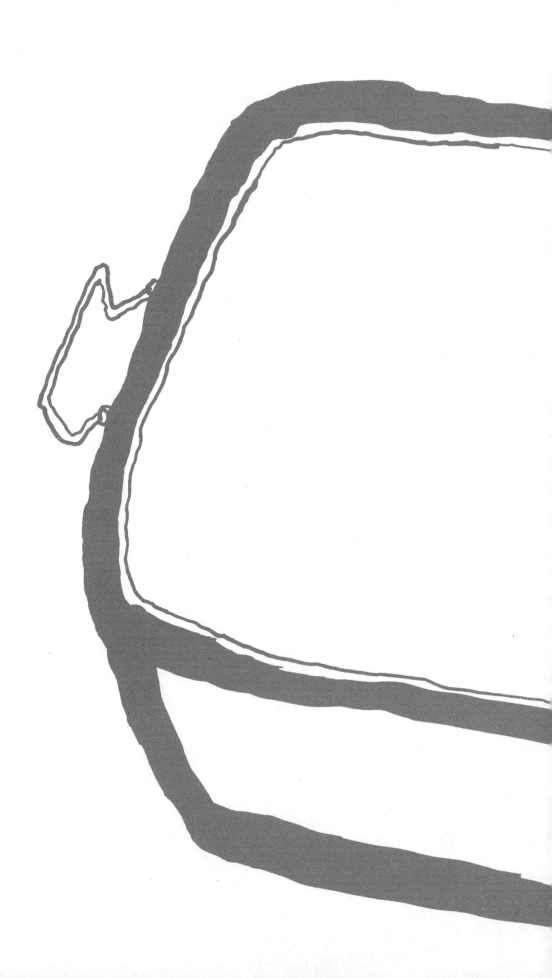

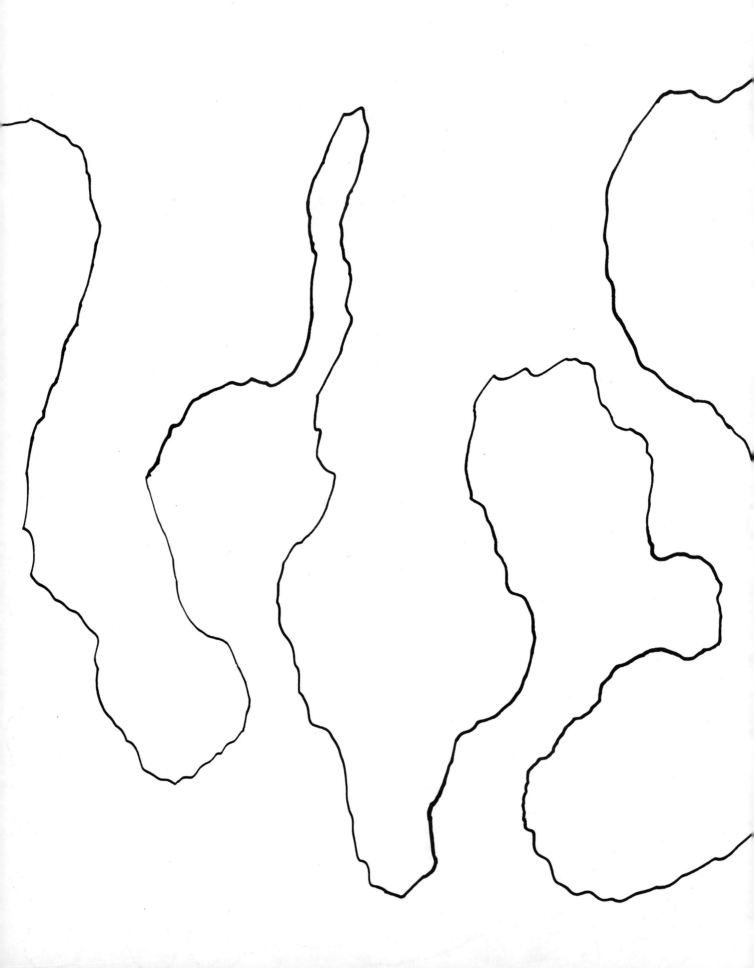

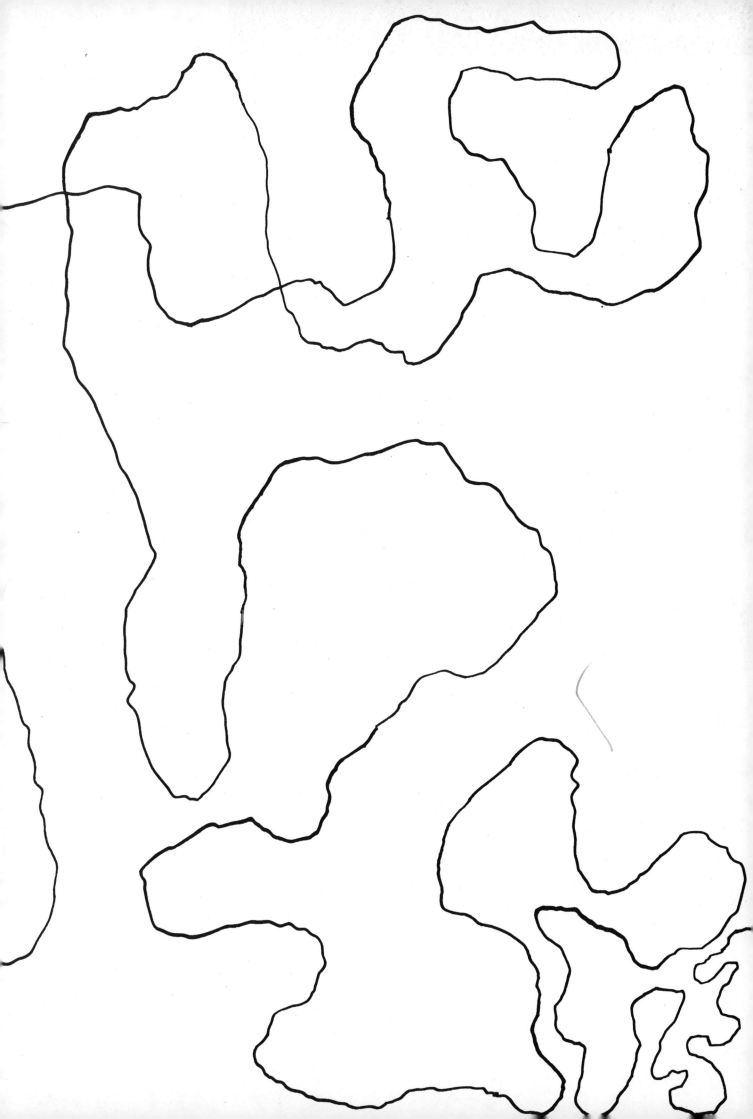

Draw some people walking down the road

And some tired people resting along the way

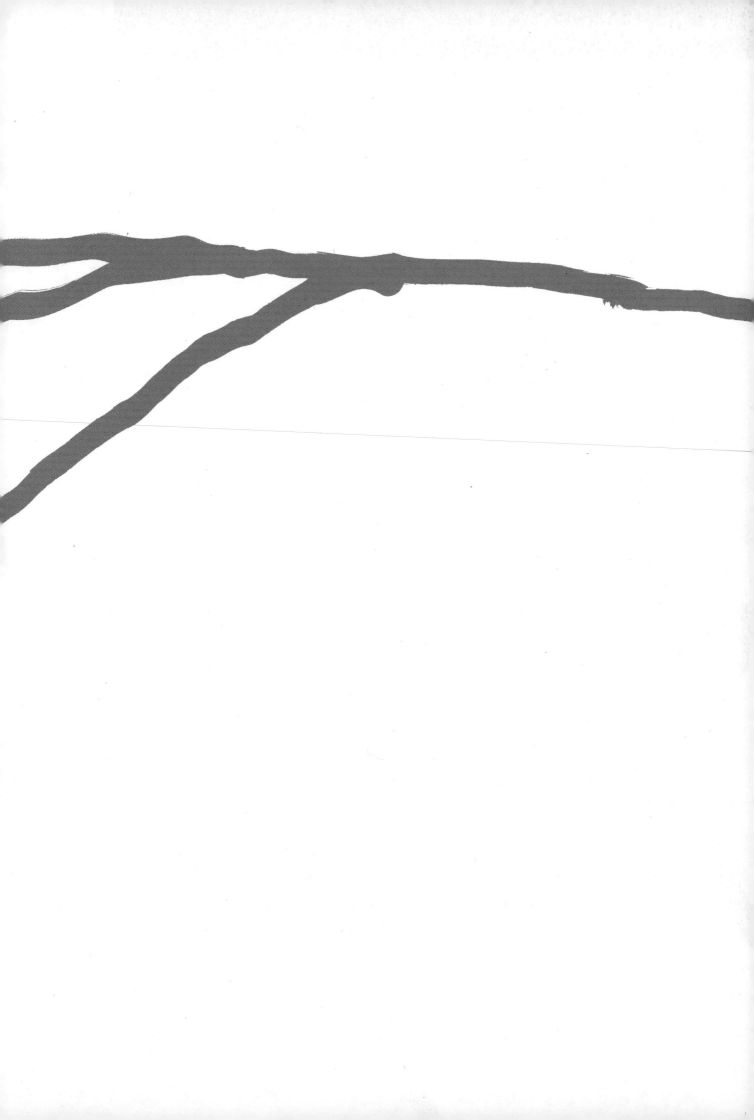

Make the lion look strong

Ouch! That hurt!

Draw bandages

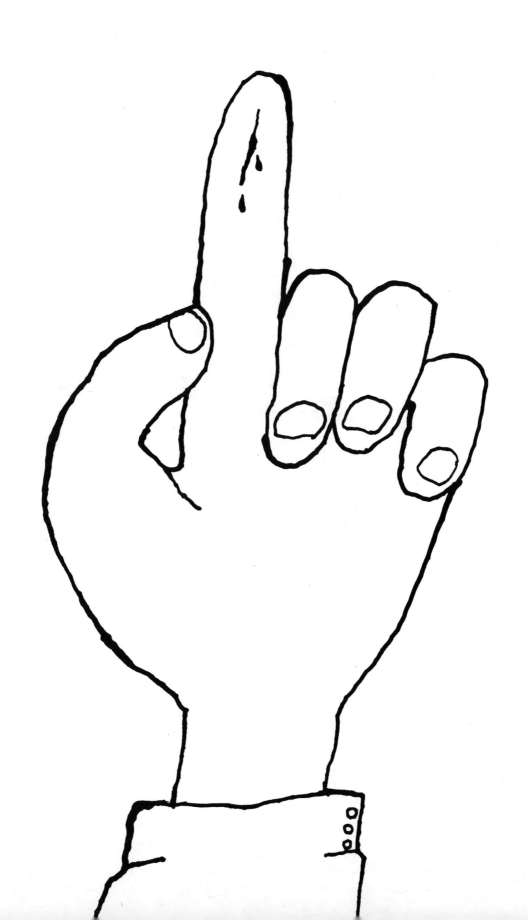

Draw some big fish

Bigger than the boat!

Find your way through the maze

ENTER

EXIT

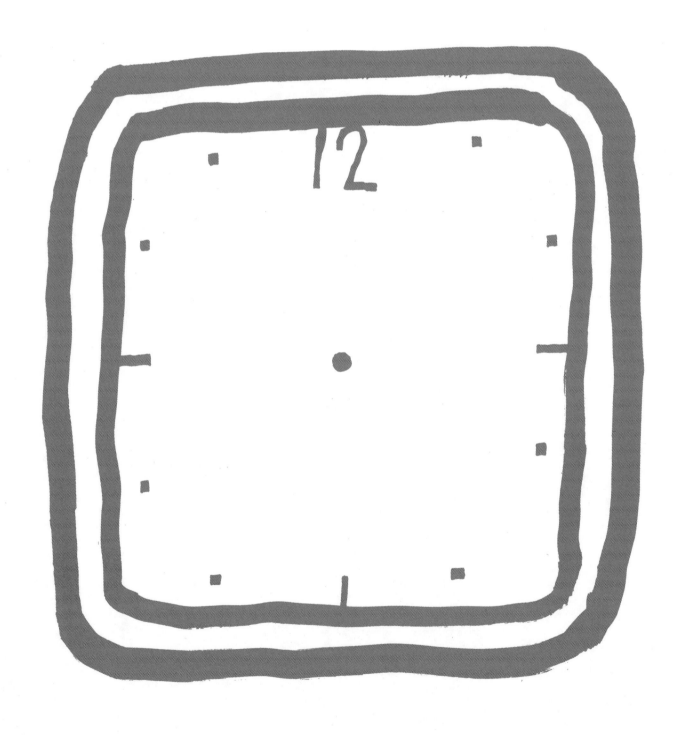

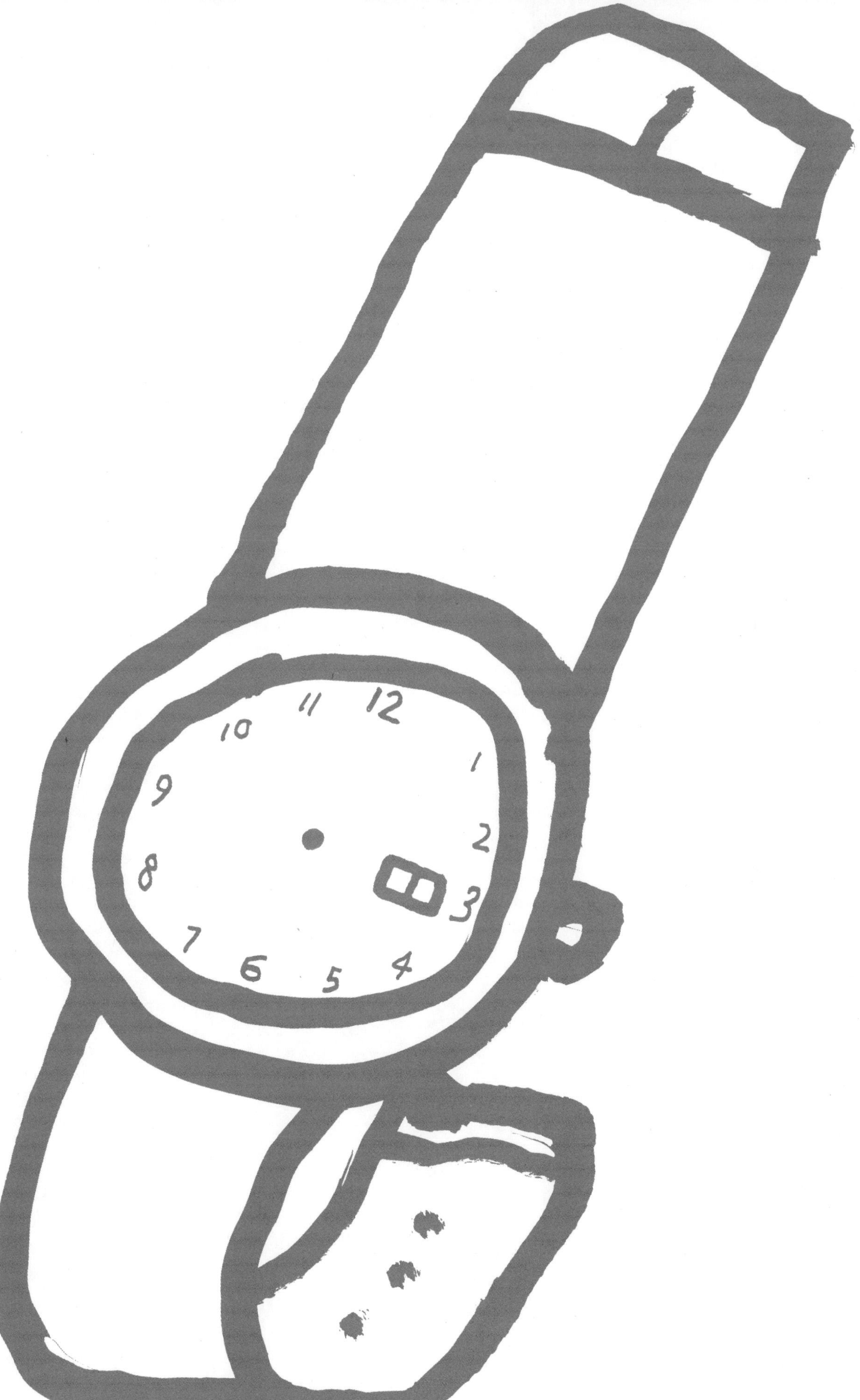
12
11
10
1
9
2
8
3
7
6
5
4

Draw laundry drying

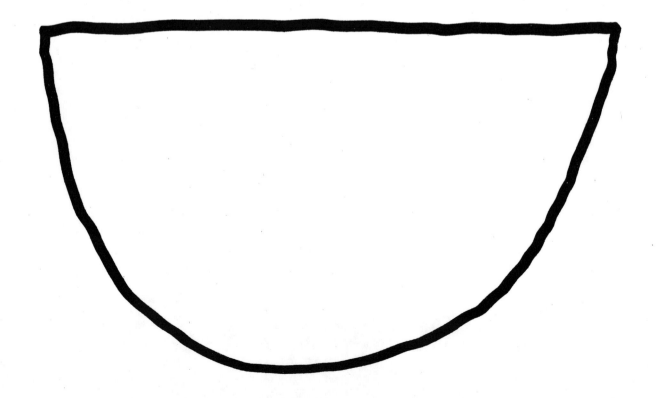

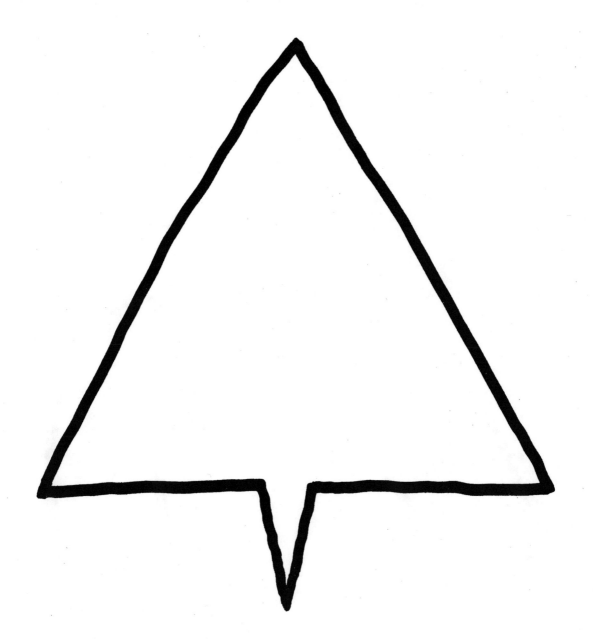

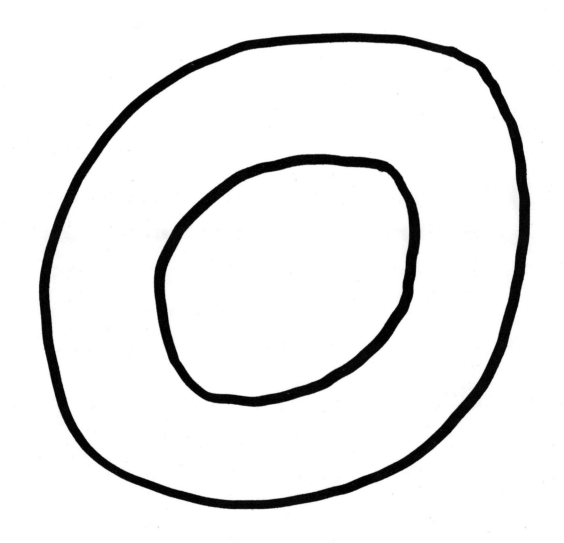

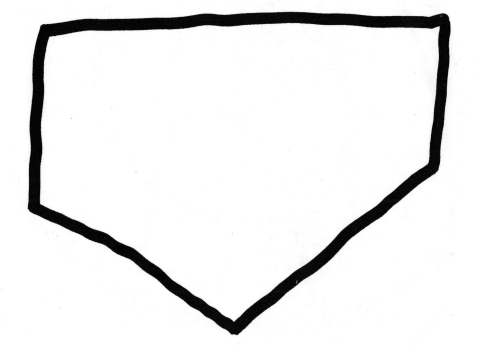

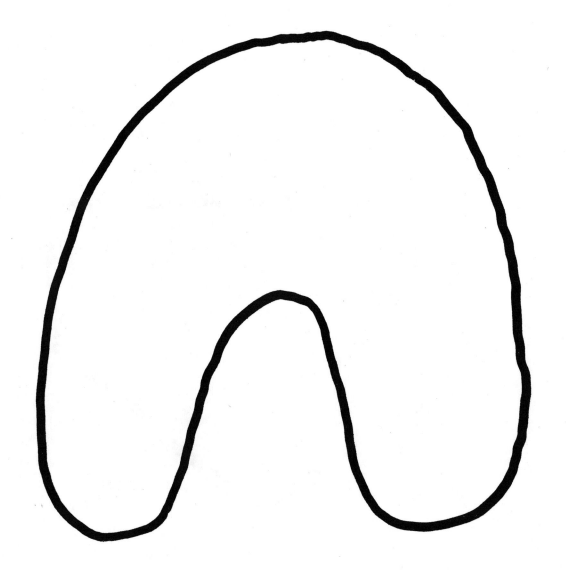

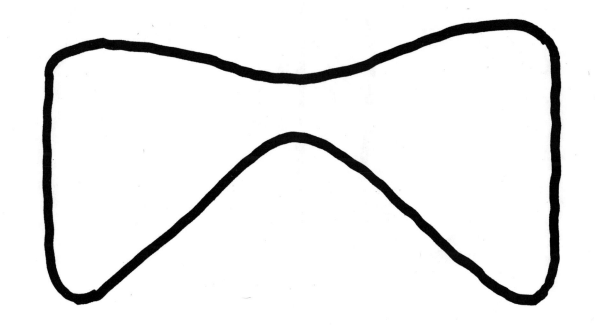

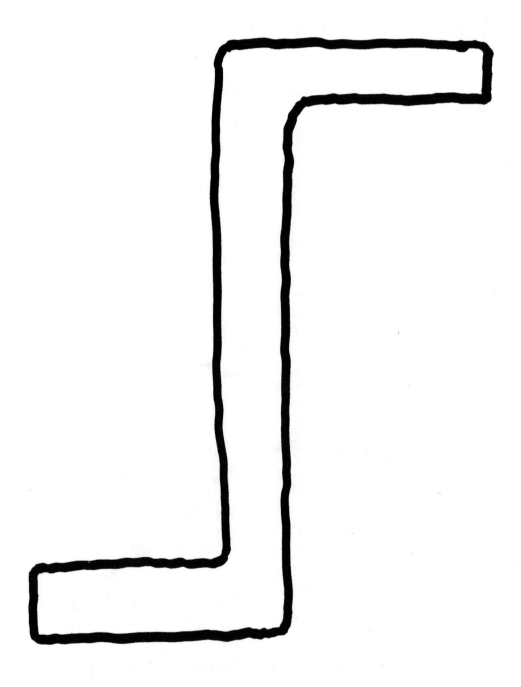

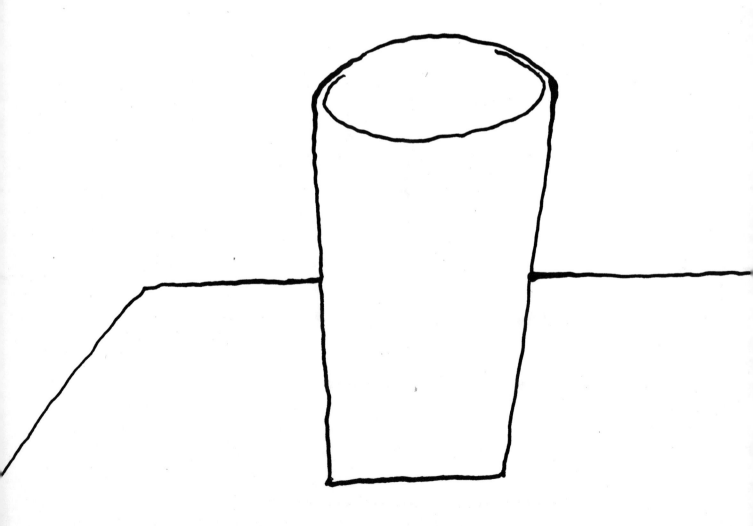

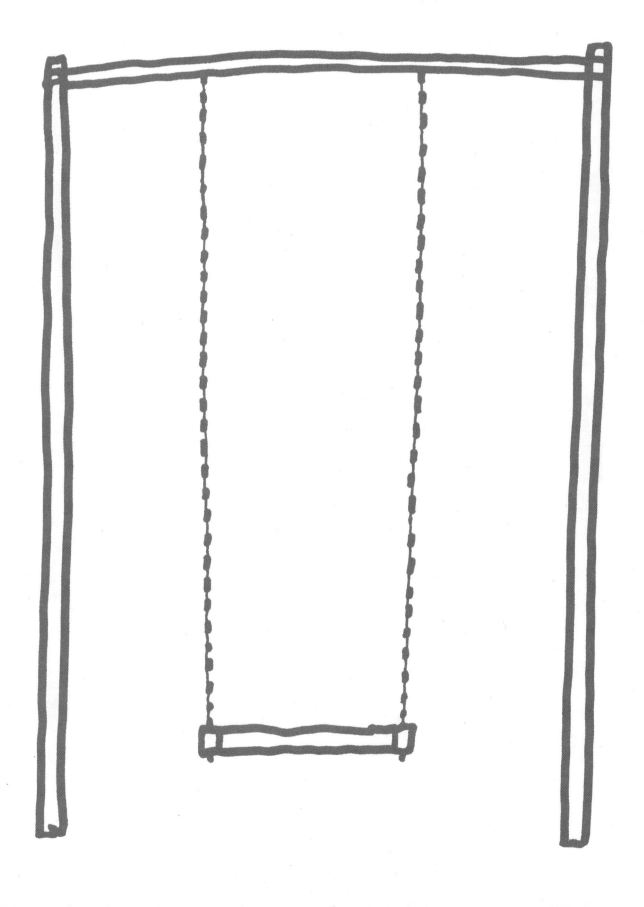

Help! A horrible dog

Draw a chick hatching

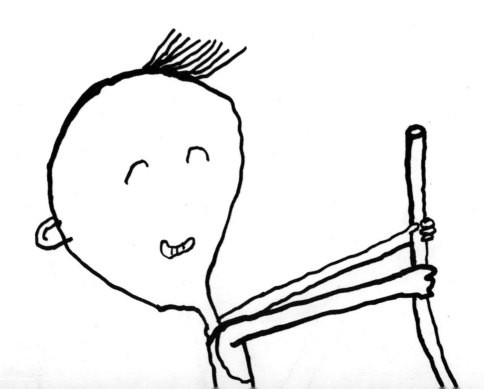

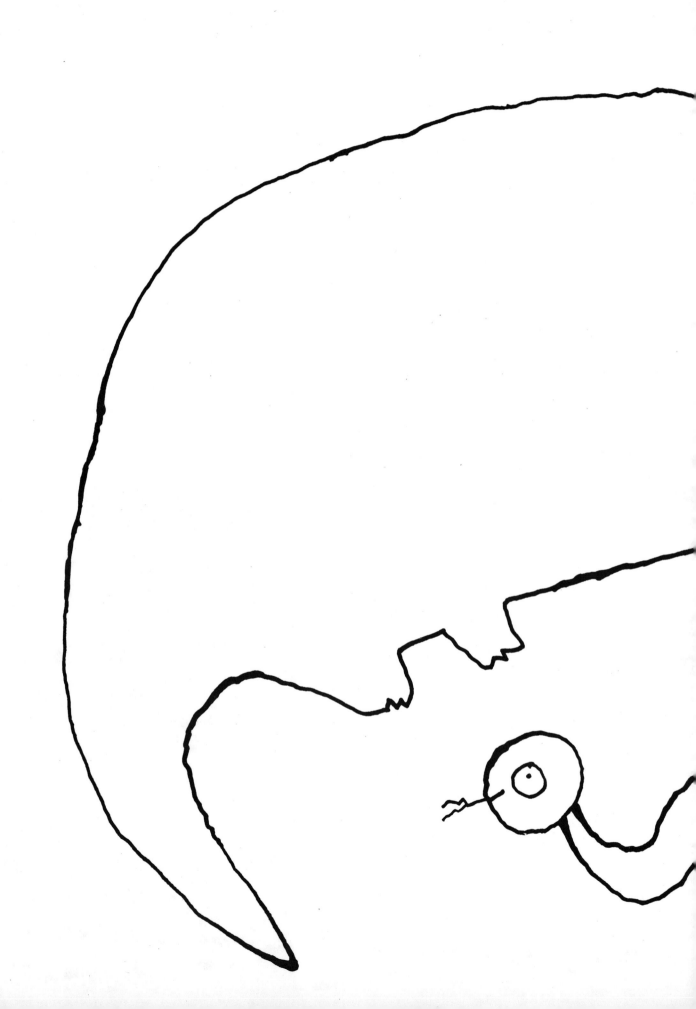

Attack the monster

Make him disappear by covering him completely

Help the bunny find his way

Draw a TV show you really like

What color is the mouse?

What color is the elephant?

Whew! It's hot!

Color the thermometer

 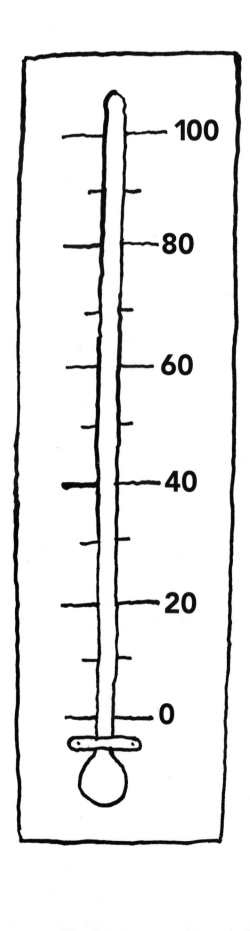

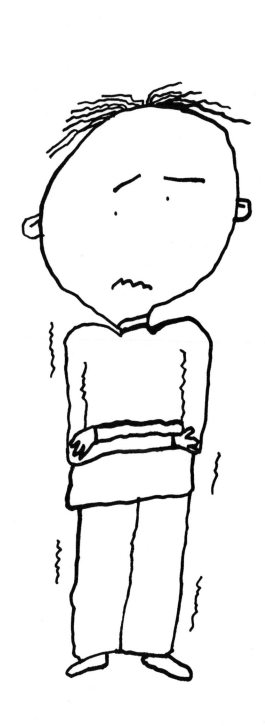

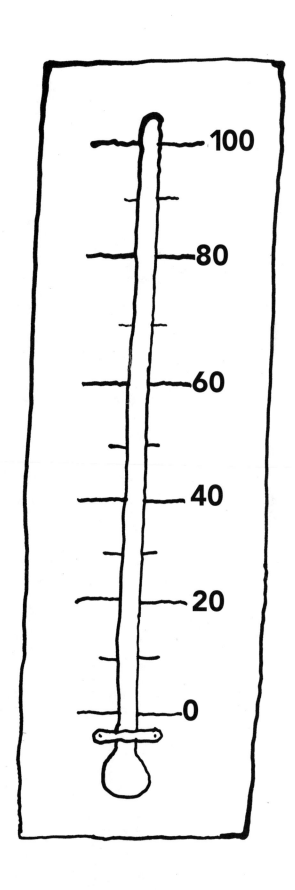

100

80

60

40

20

0

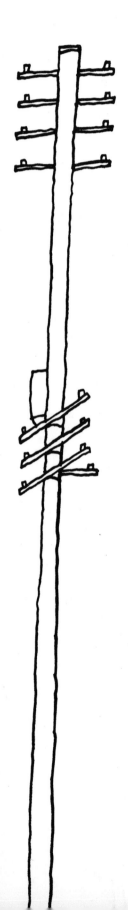

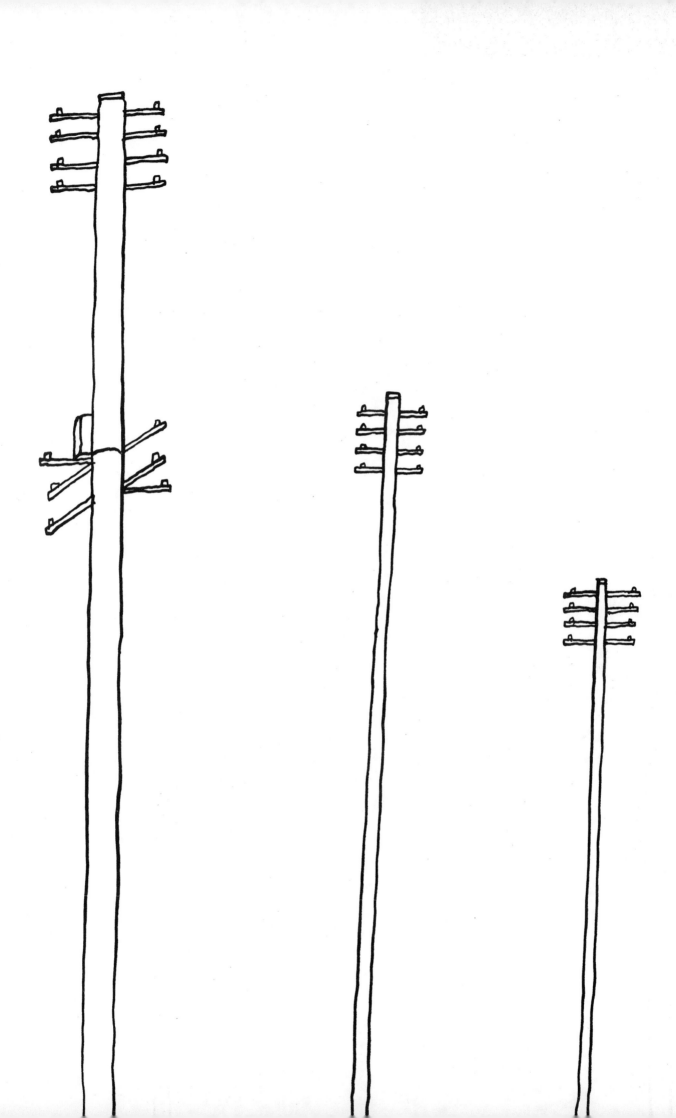

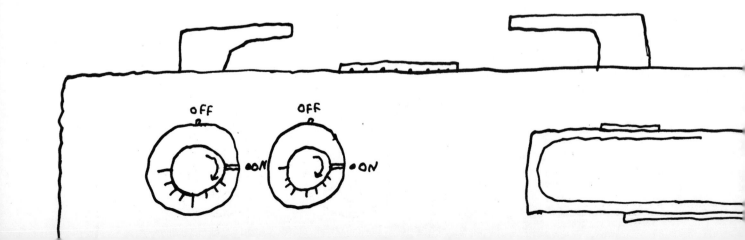

OFF

OFF

ON

ON

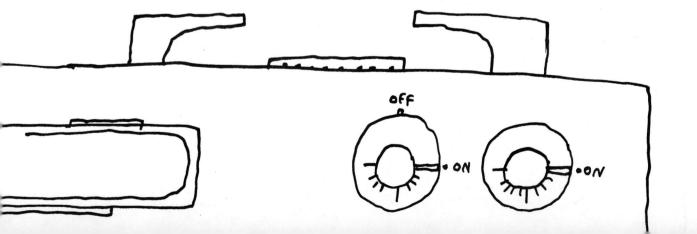

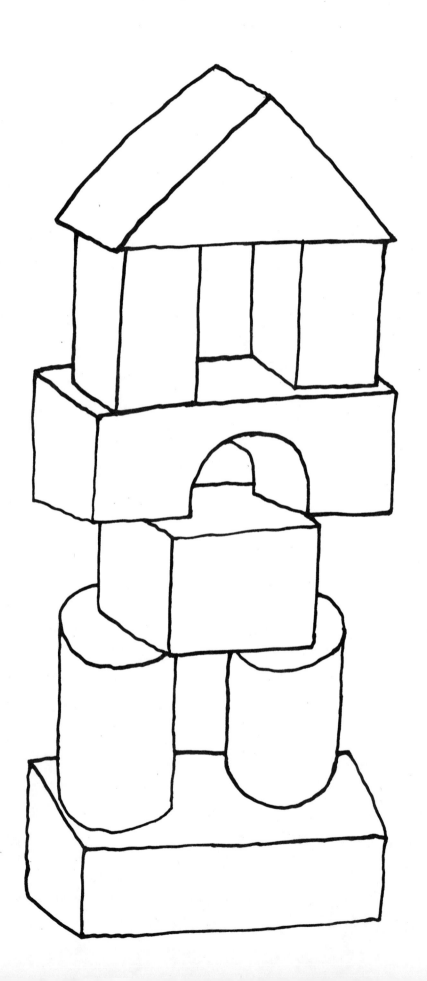

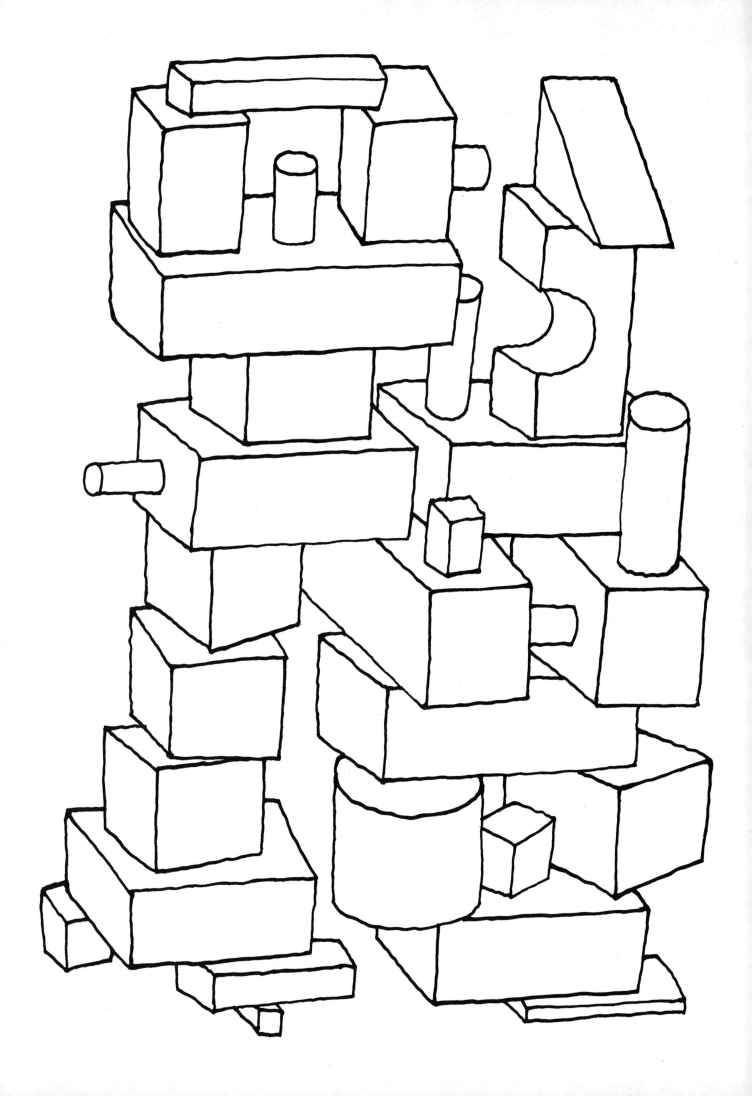

This is a mountain of sugar

Draw ants marching

Draw babies

Make them as cute as you can

Draw a racecourse around these flags

Go around all of the flags

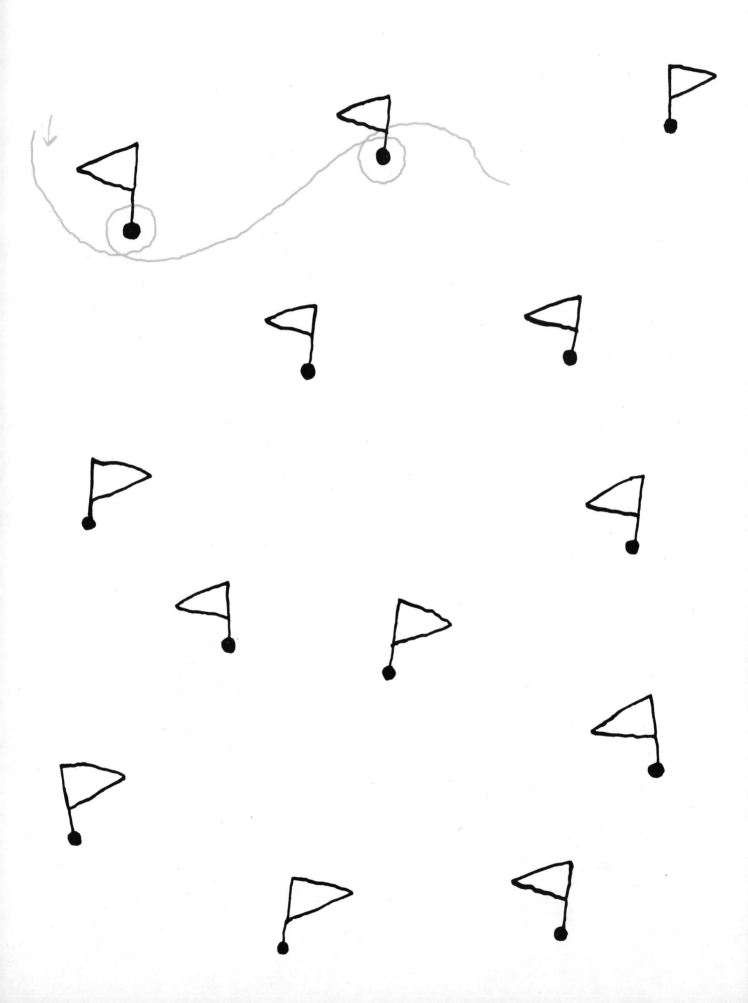

It's Christmas!

Decorate the tree and light the candle

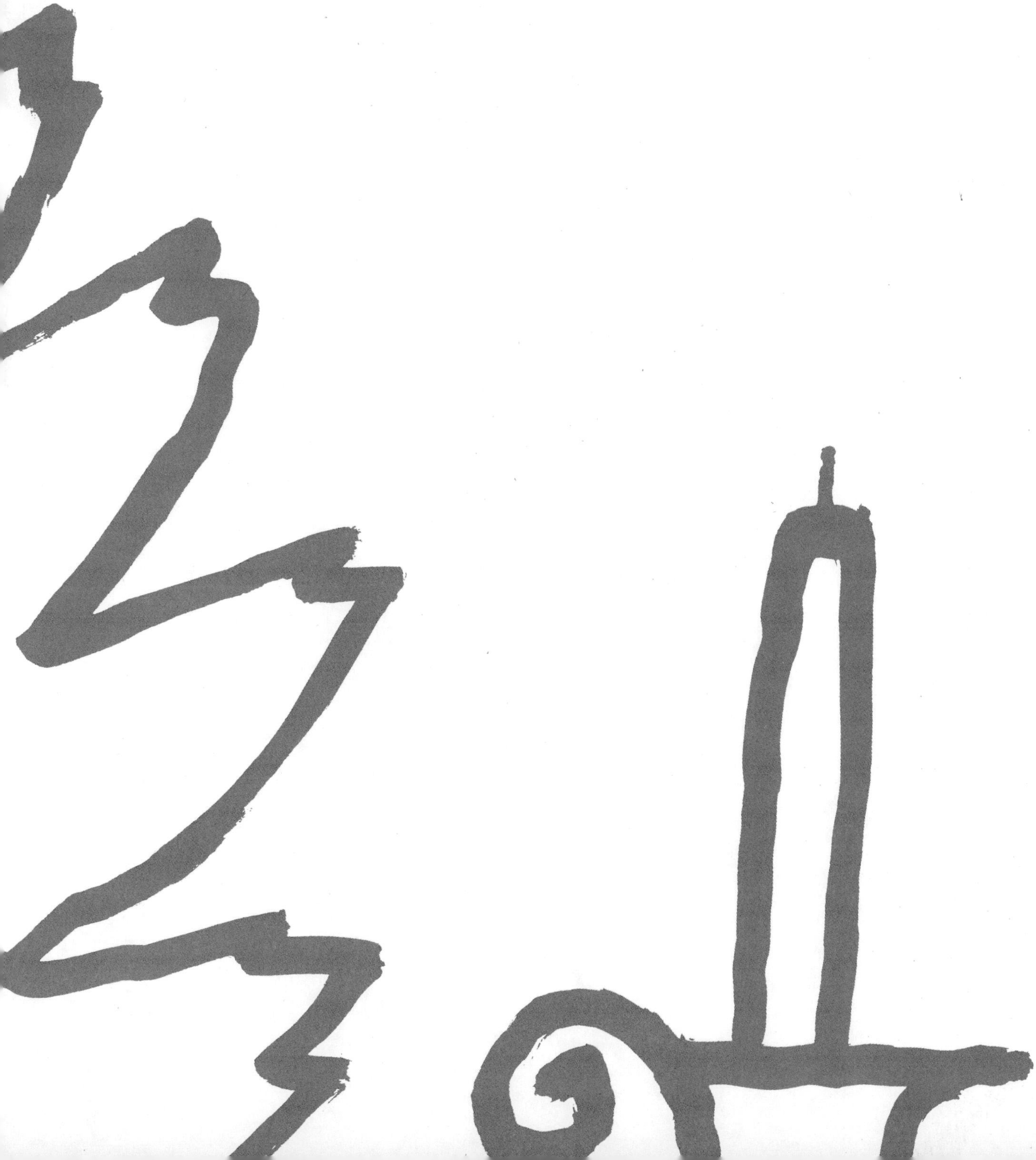

Draw 2 clowns

One on the ball and one on the horse

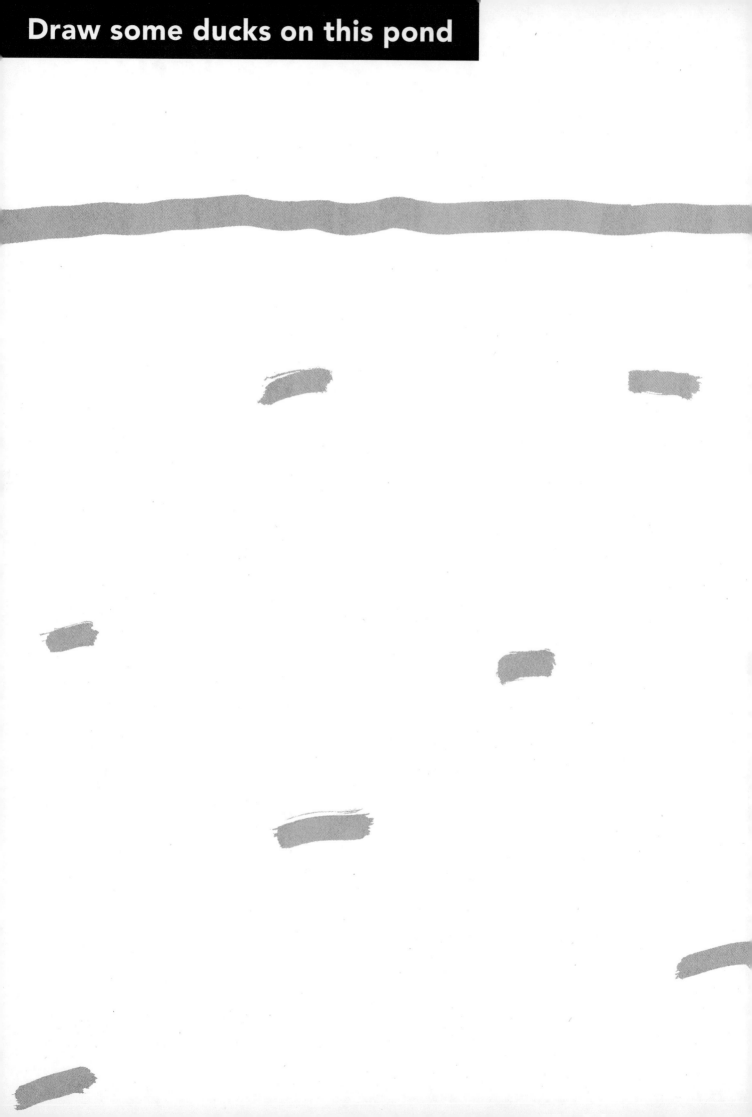

Draw some ducks on this pond

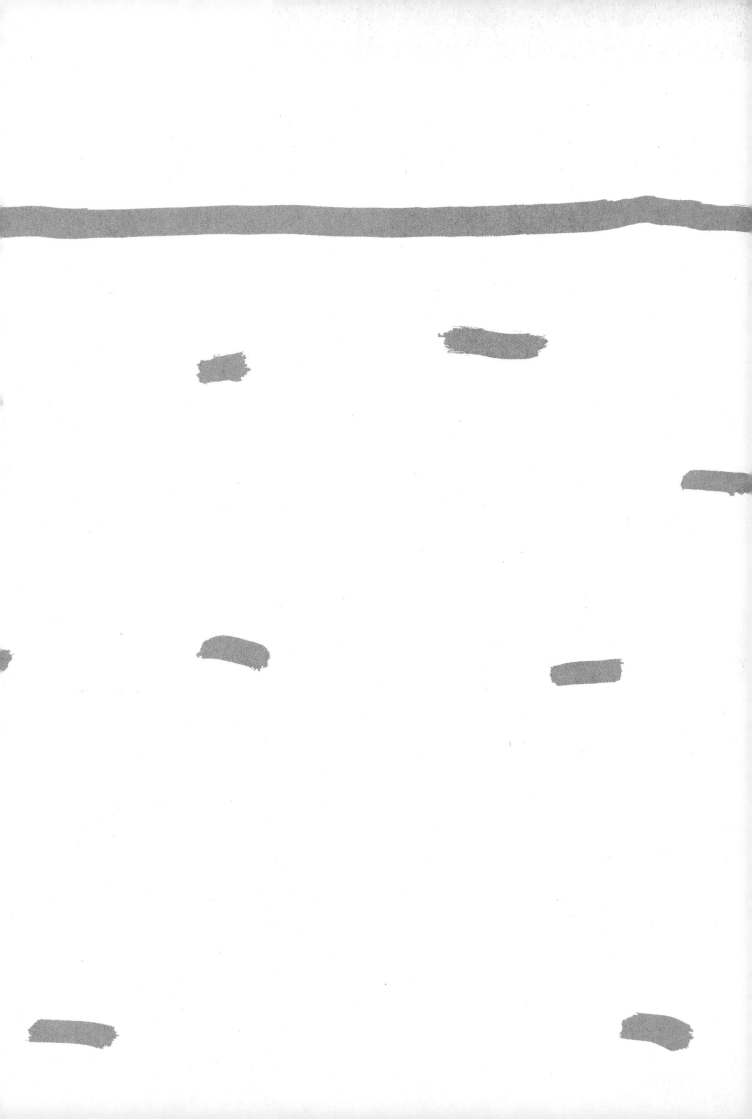

This penguin is very cold

How can you warm him up?

This owl is very tired

Draw him a bed to sleep in

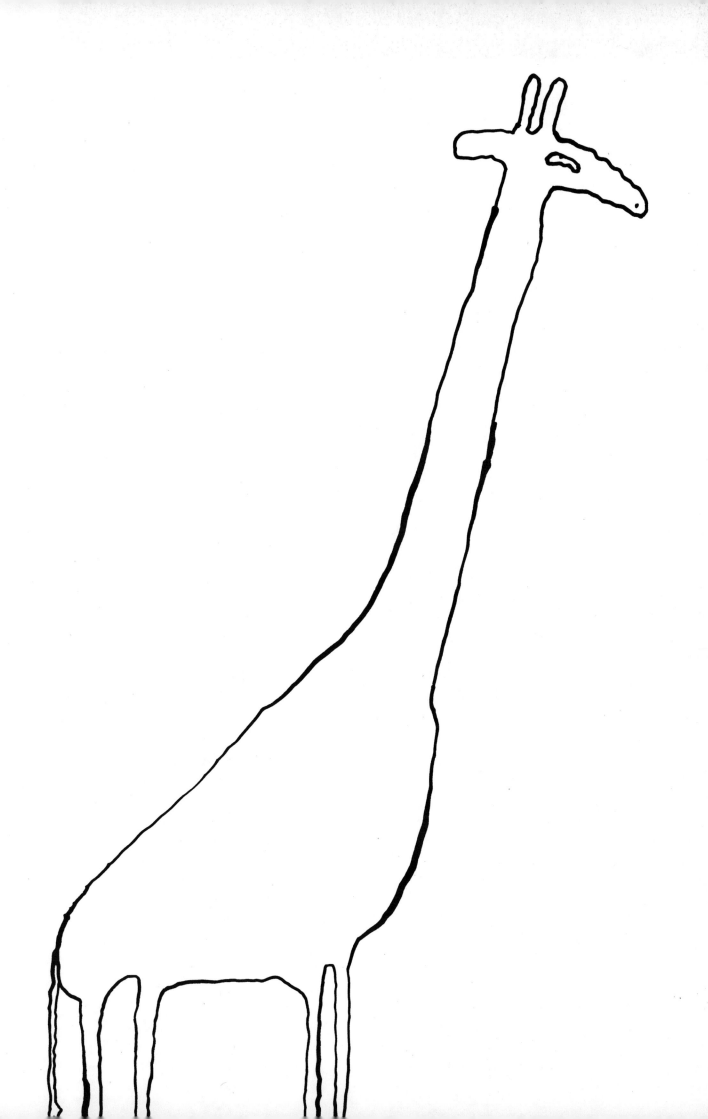

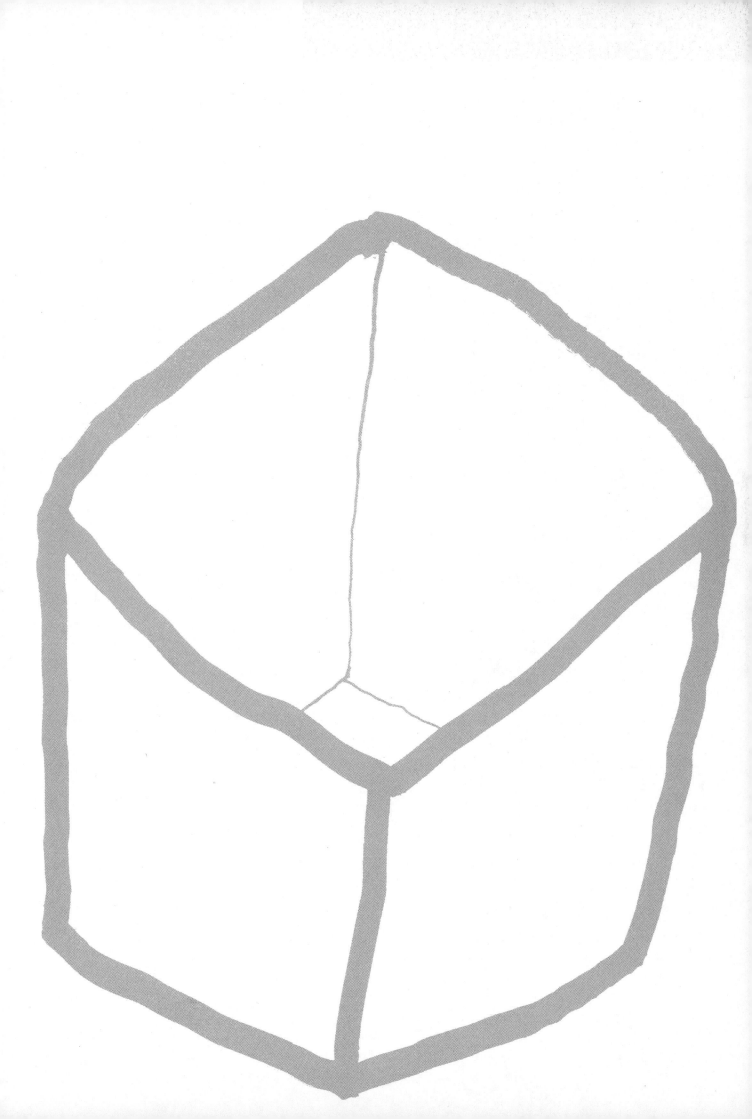

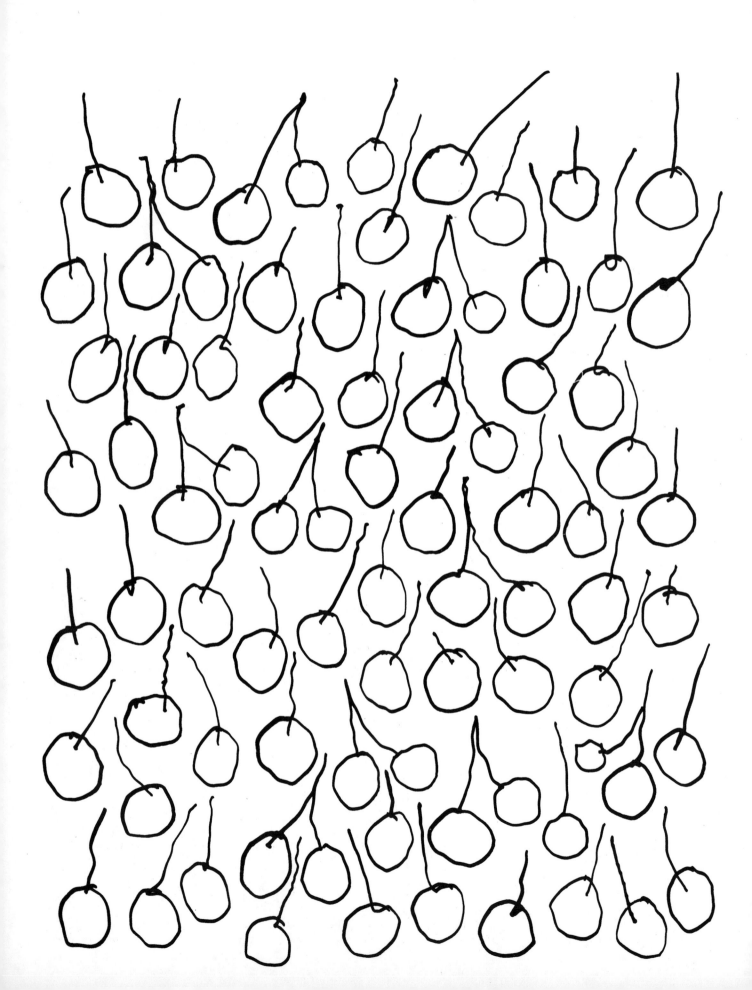

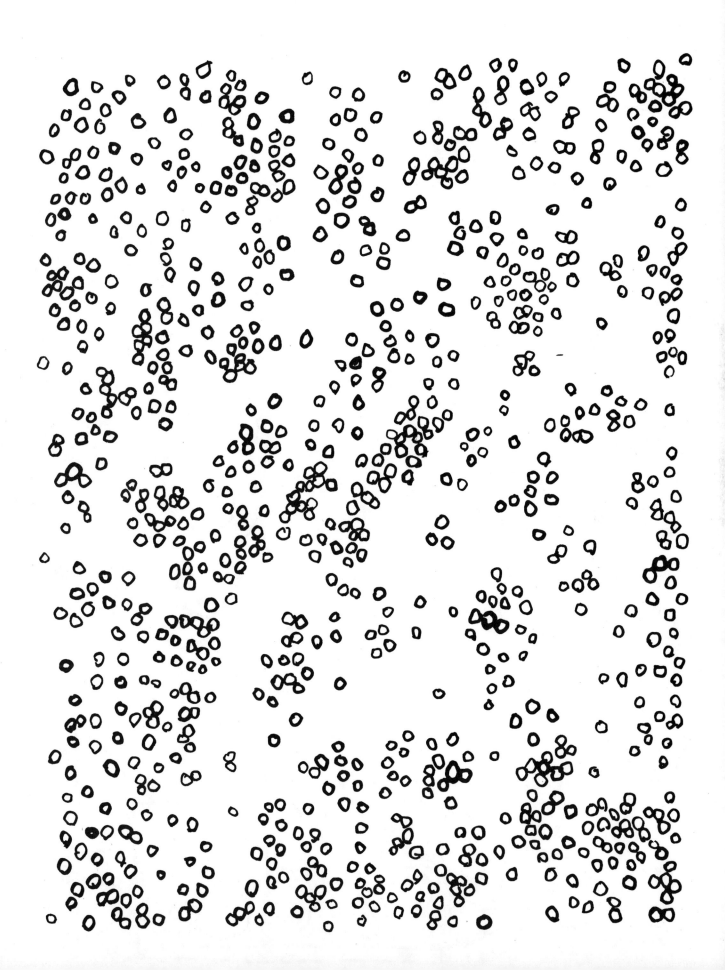

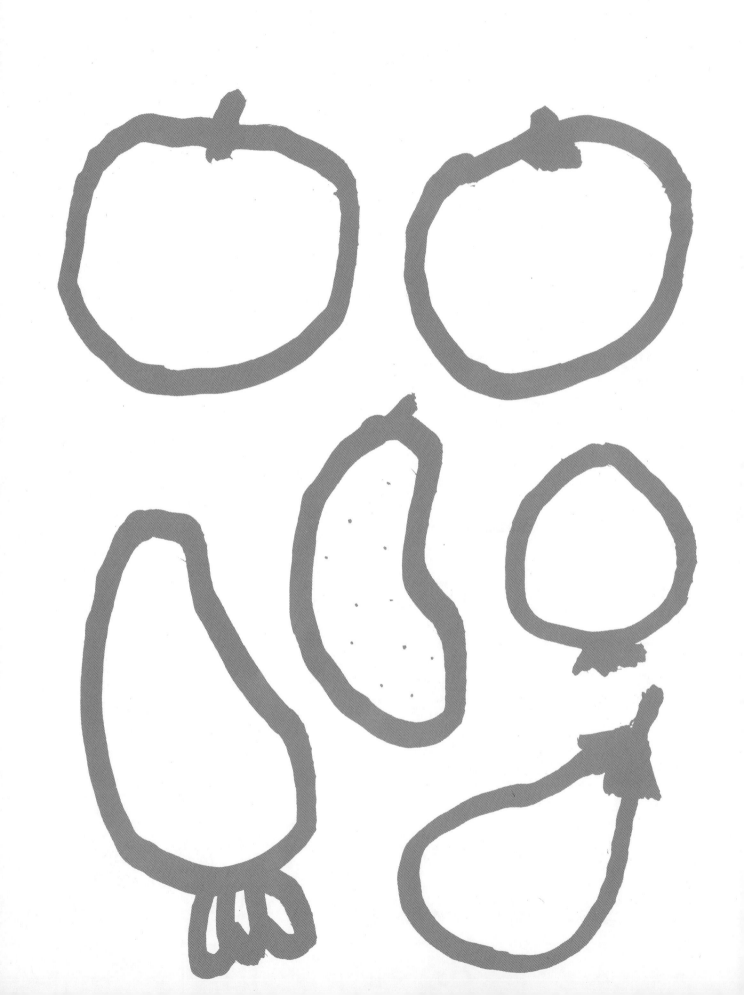

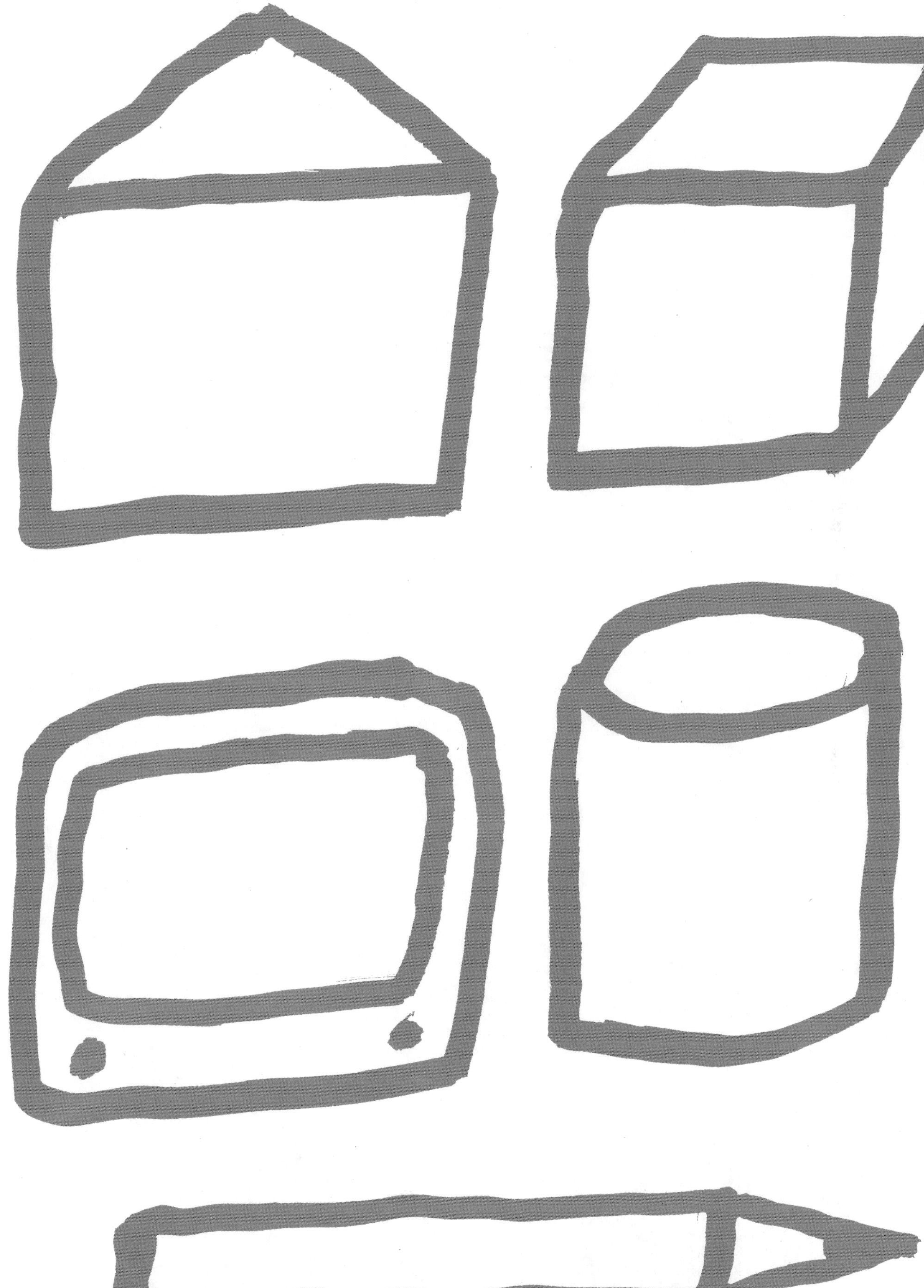

Make these two look more friendly

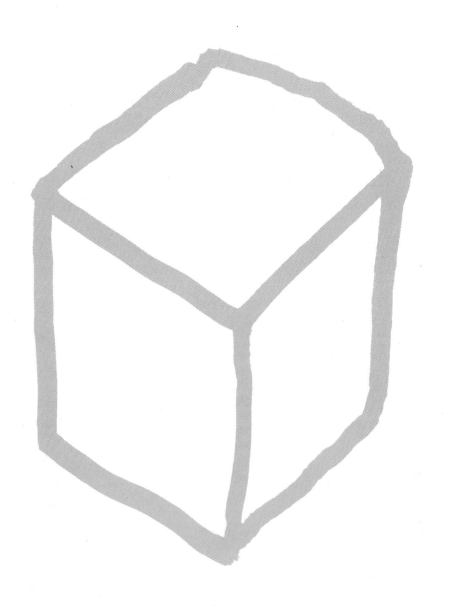

Draw a few more astronauts

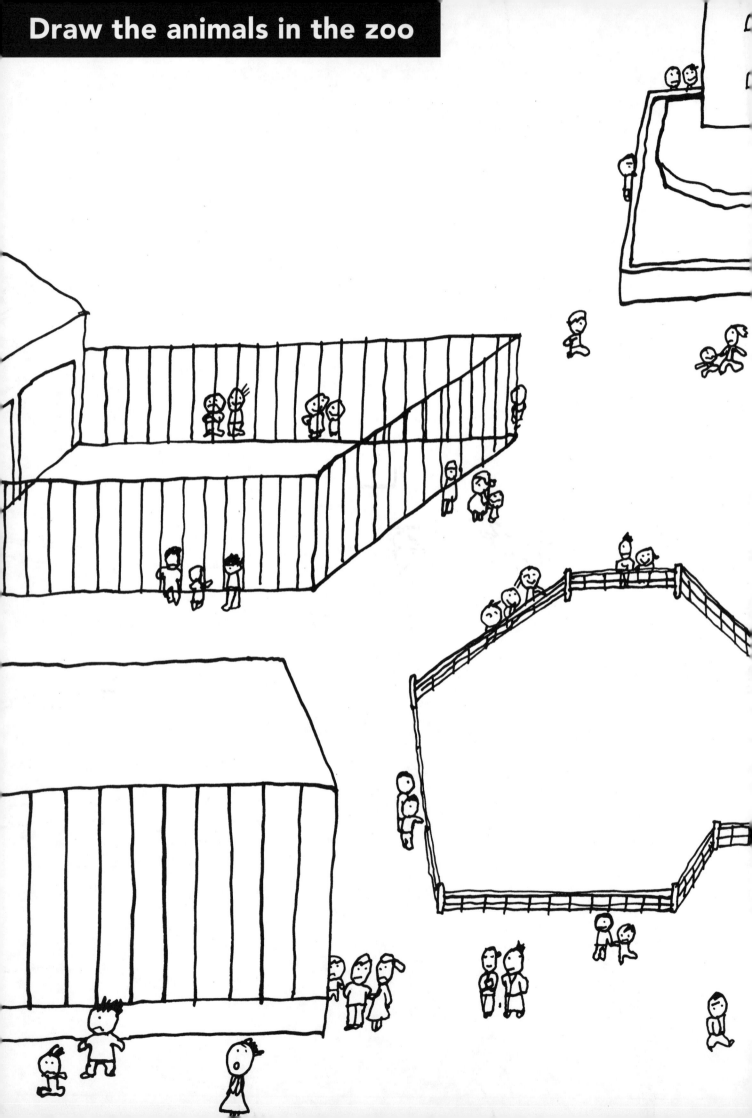

Draw the animals in the zoo

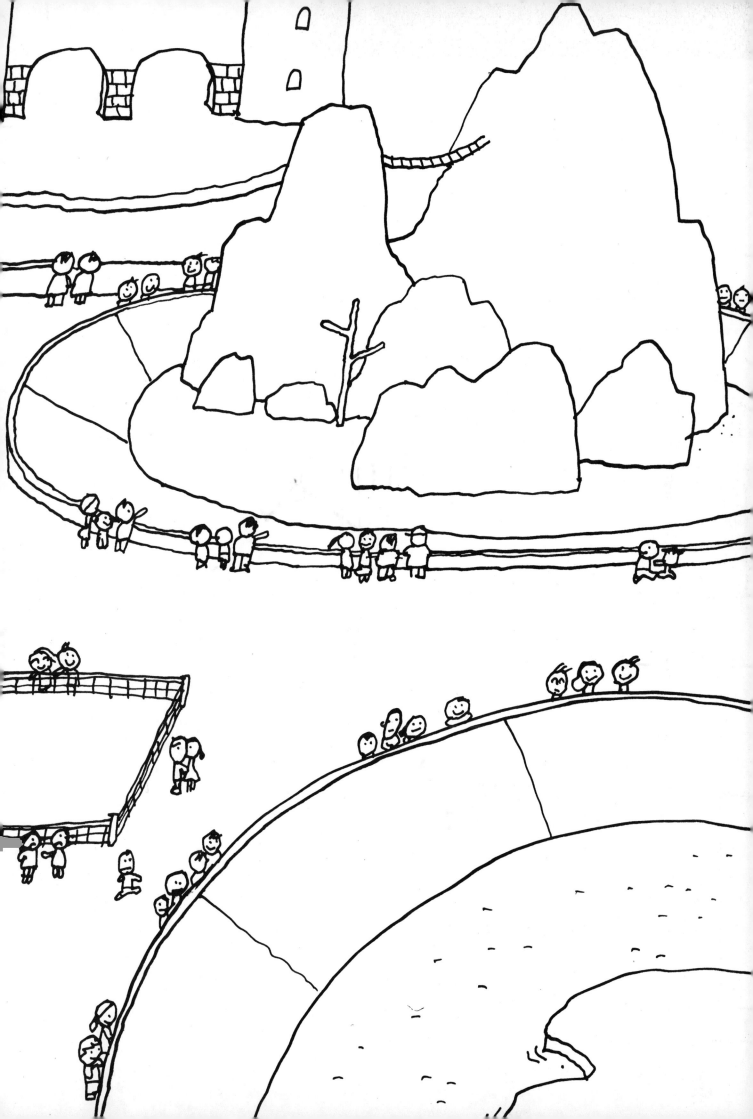

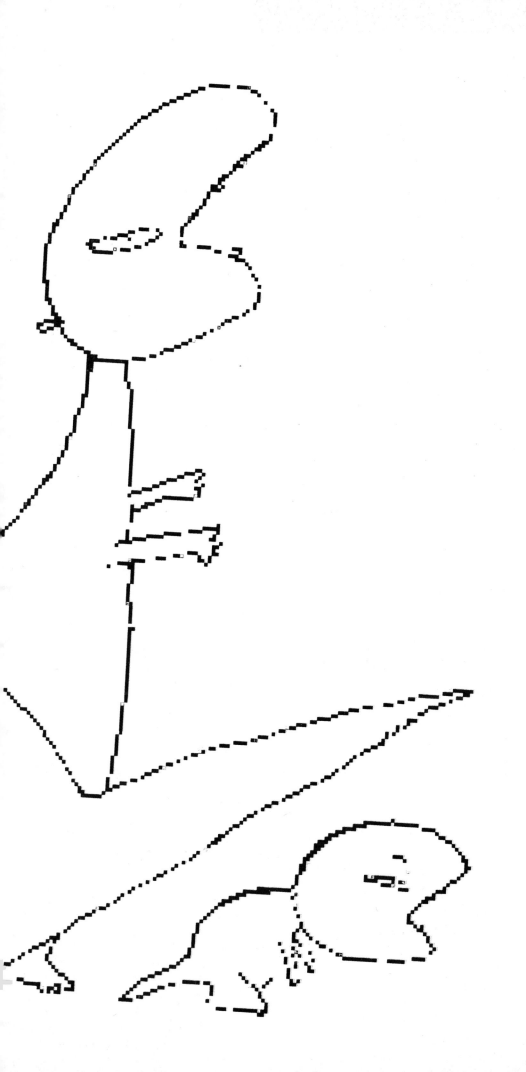

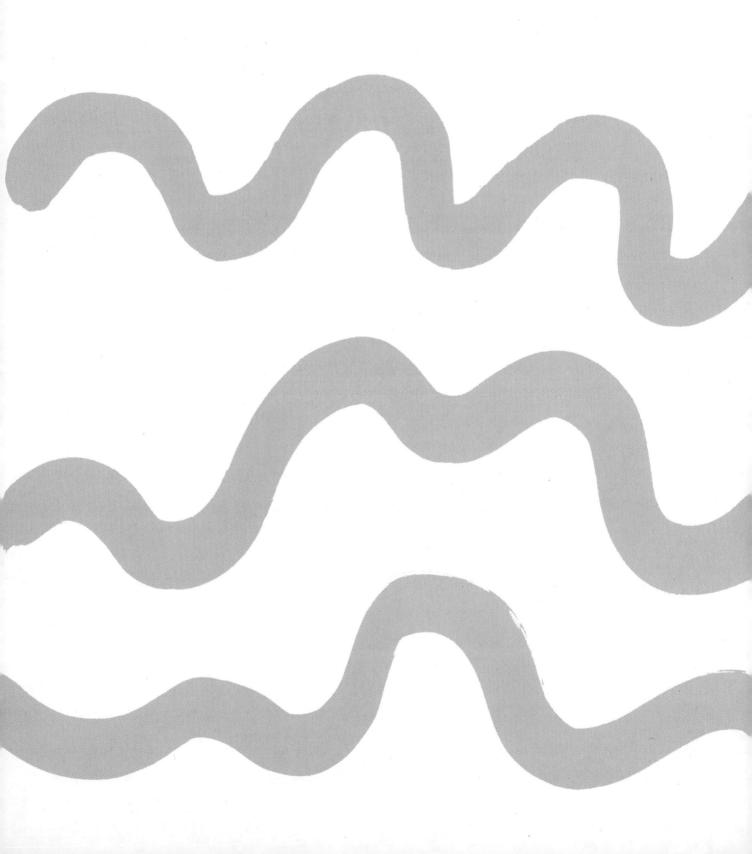

Back of the box

To make a box, cut along the dark lines, fold along the lighter lines, and glue down the tabs

You might want to color it first

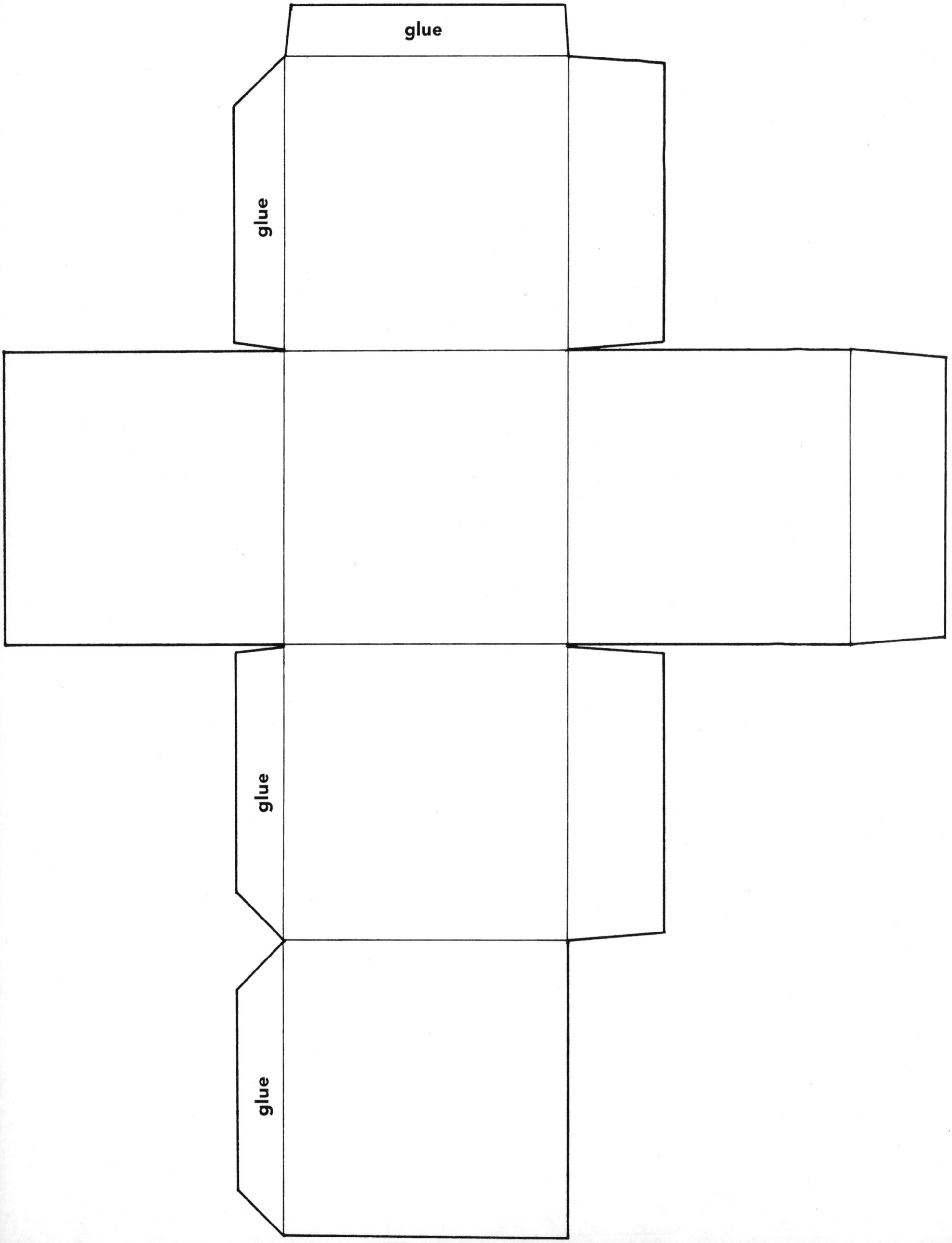

glue

glue

glue

glue

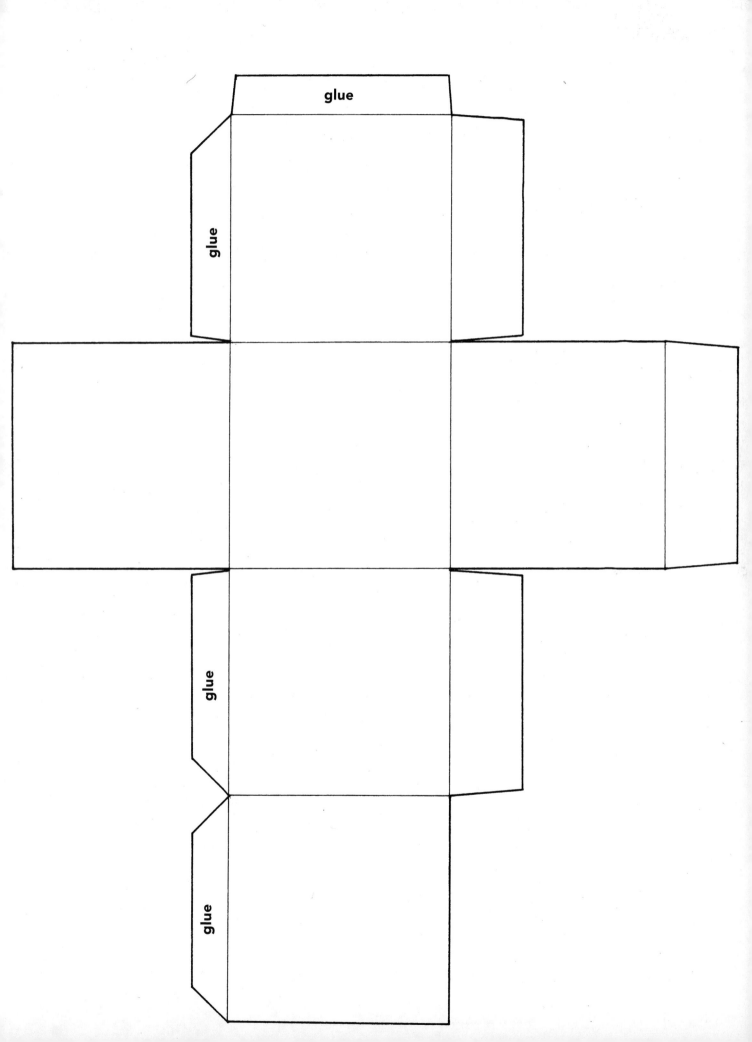

Back of the box

If it becomes too difficult, stop!

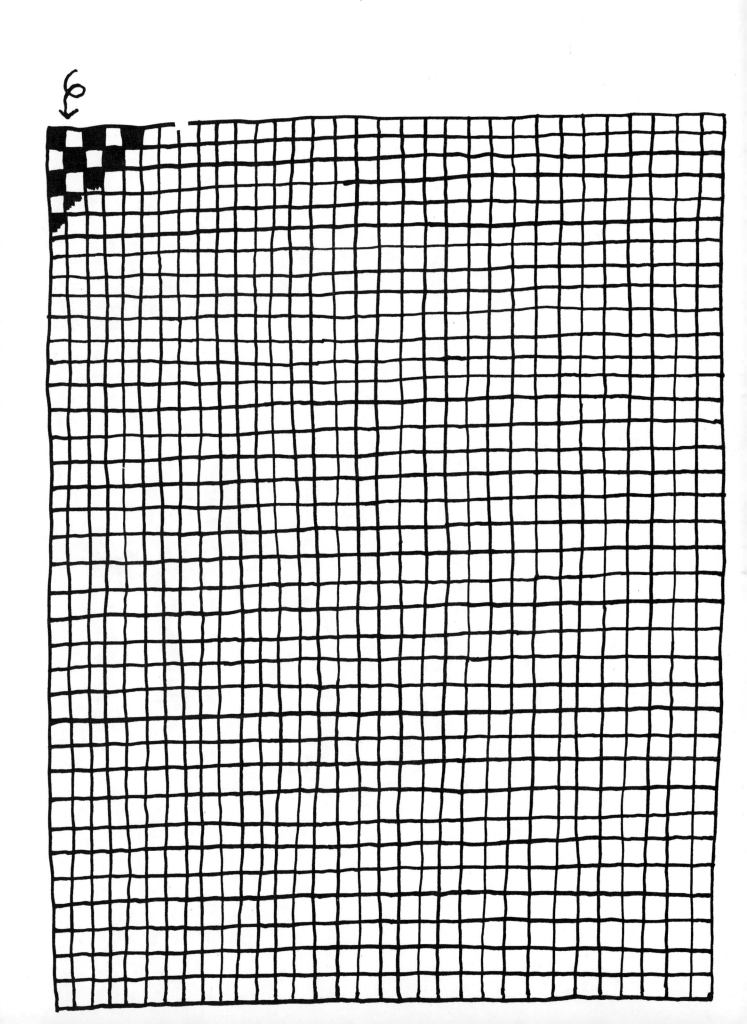

This is a tiger

Draw its stripes

This is a panther

Draw its black fur

This is a leopard

Draw its spots

Draw lots of stars

This is the jungle

Draw all the animals that are hiding

Back of the mask

Color them and cut them out

Back of the mask

Back of the mask

Back of the mask

Back of the mask

The sun and a star

Scribble on this wall

Hurry up or you might get caught!

This is a mountain

Draw some mountain climbers

Correct them

To day, be cause the wether was not naice, my father and i went to the moovies. After that, we brought some post cards in a toi shoppe. We were veri pleesed. Tommorrow, the wether wount to be nice eithir.

This is a bowl of soup

Draw the ingredients

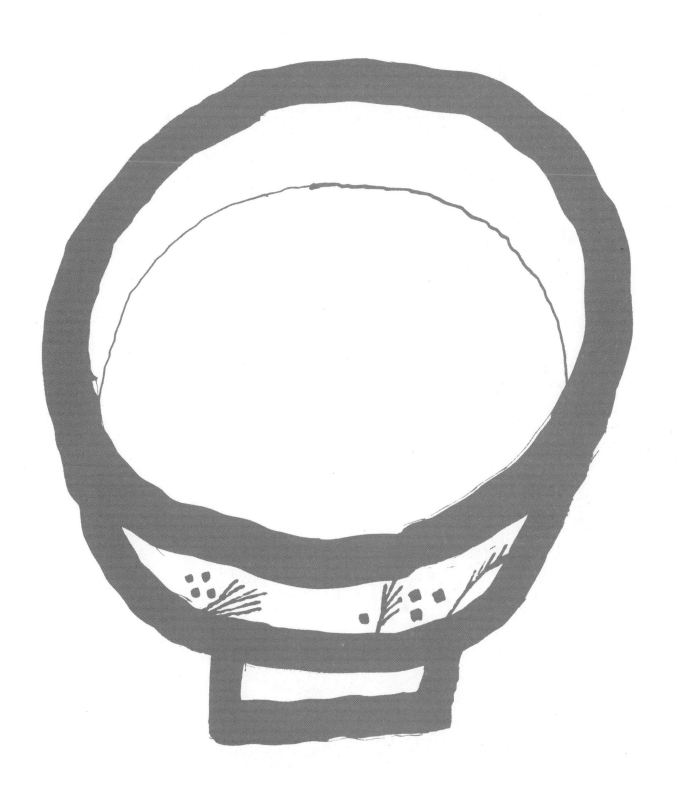

Calendar

Monday	Tuesday	Wednesday	Thursday	Friday	Saturday	Sunday

CALENDAR.

日　　月　　火　　水　　木　　金　　土
SUN.　MON.　TUE.　WED.　THU.　FRI.　SAT.

This is a forest

Draw the animals hiding among the trees

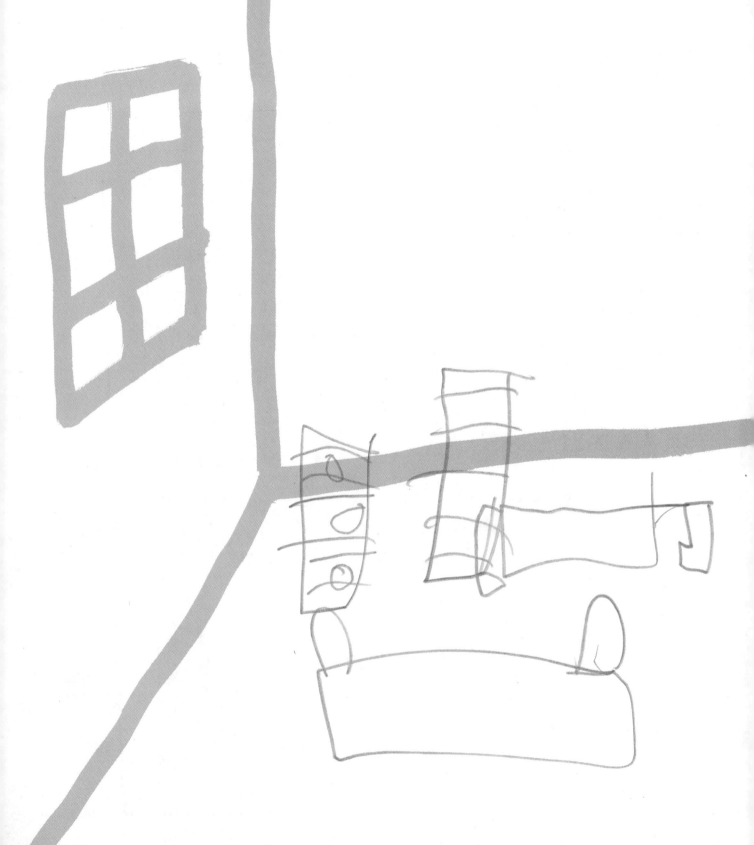

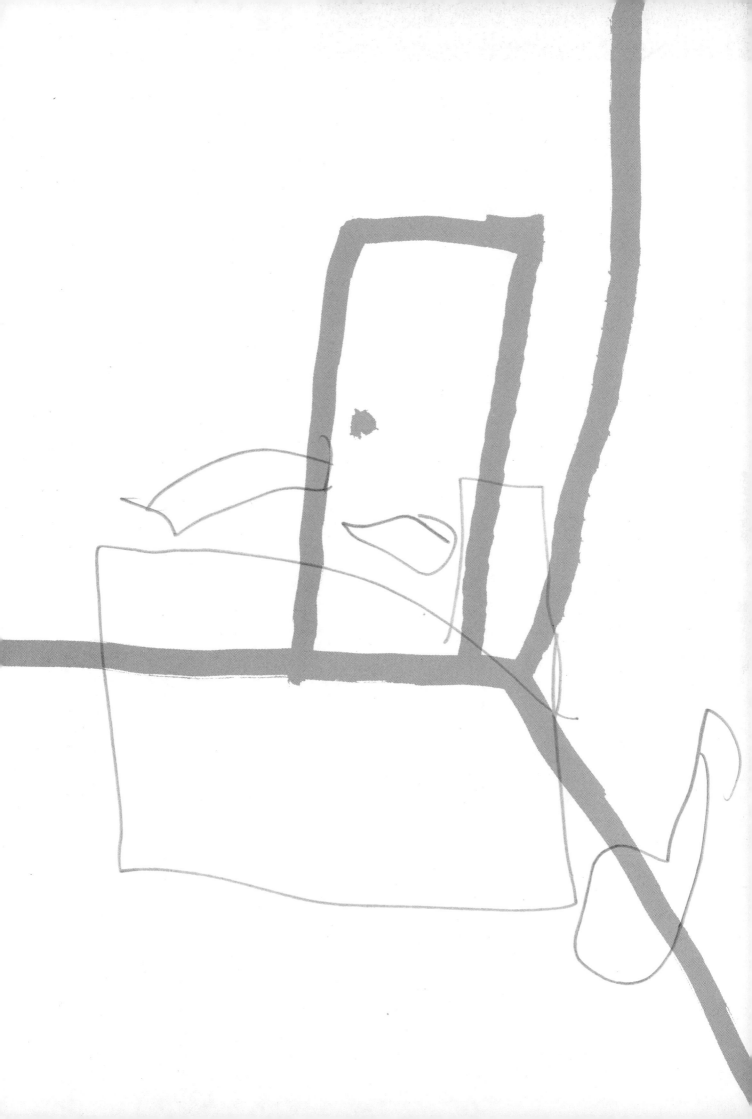

Draw on these empty canvasses

Imagine what these people would paint

Draw people walking around

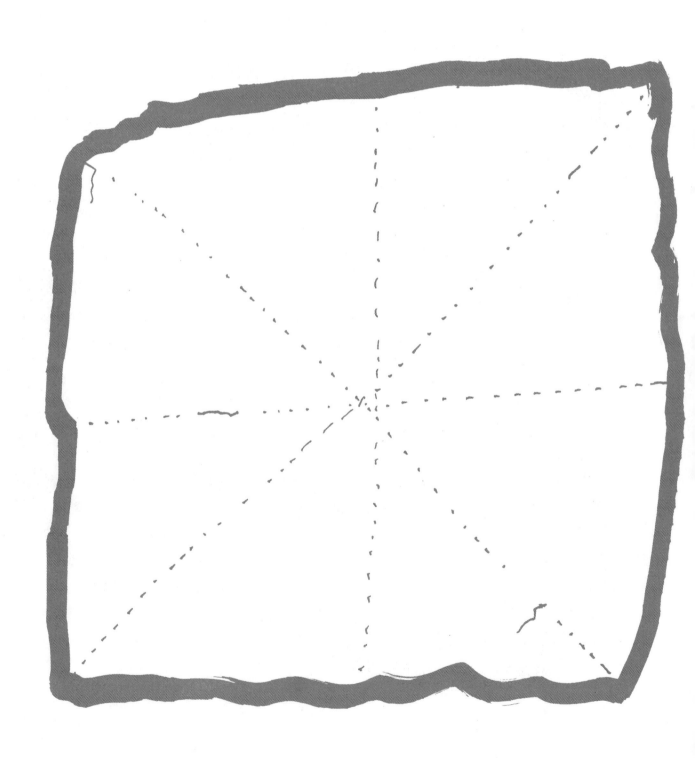

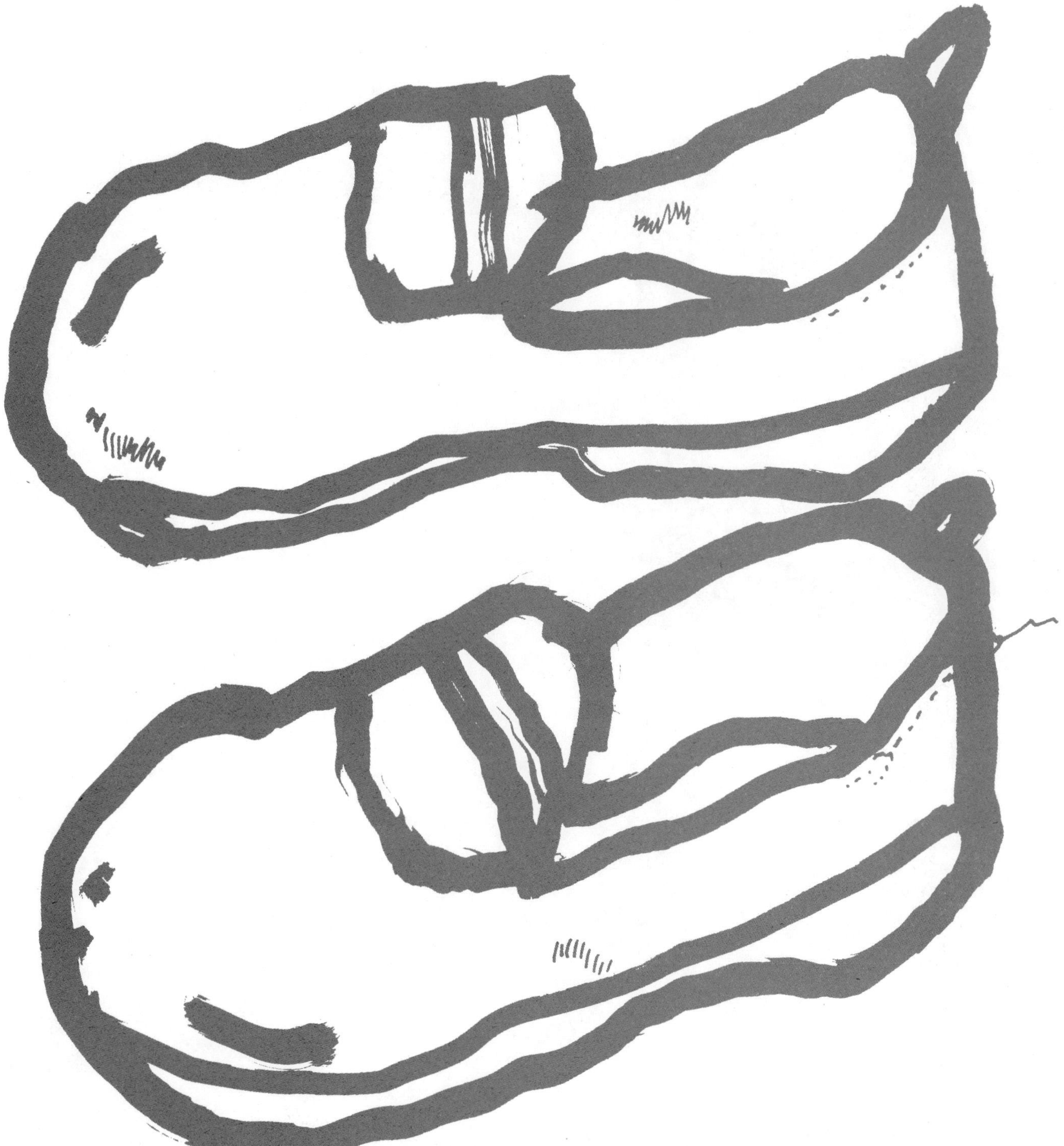

Draw lots of gravy, too

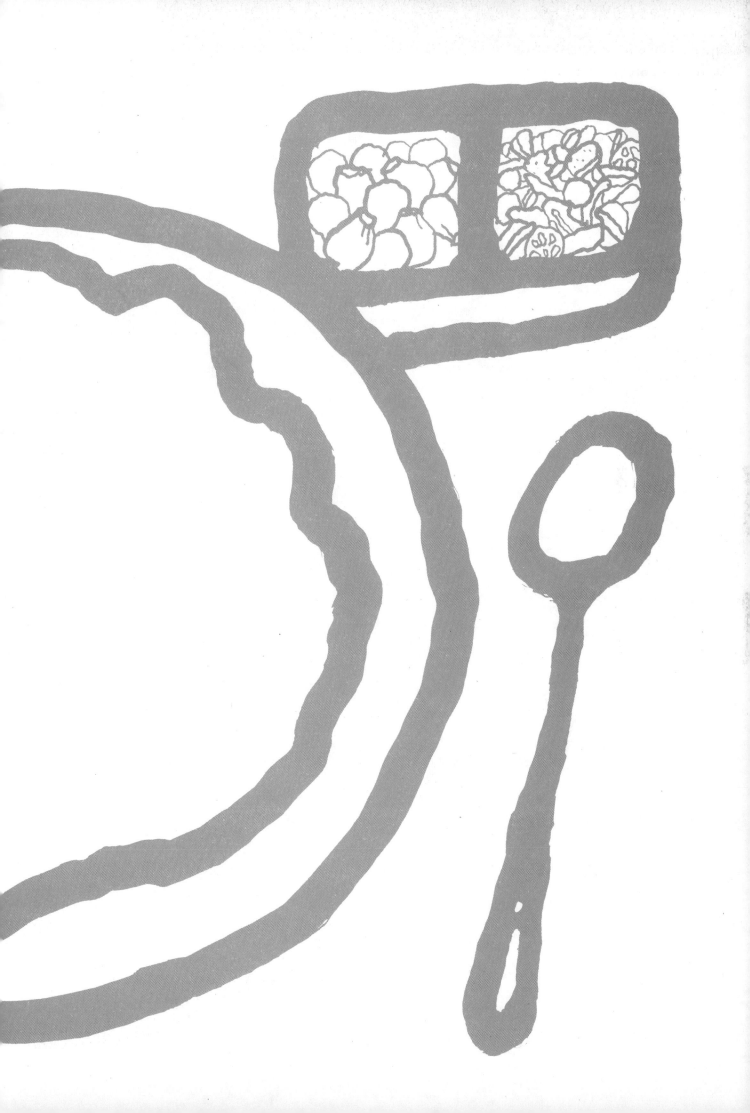

Wham! It's a fly ball!

Draw the person who's going to catch the ball

These are cherry trees in bloom

Draw the people who have come to admire them

What's on the ground here?

Make these pastries look delicious

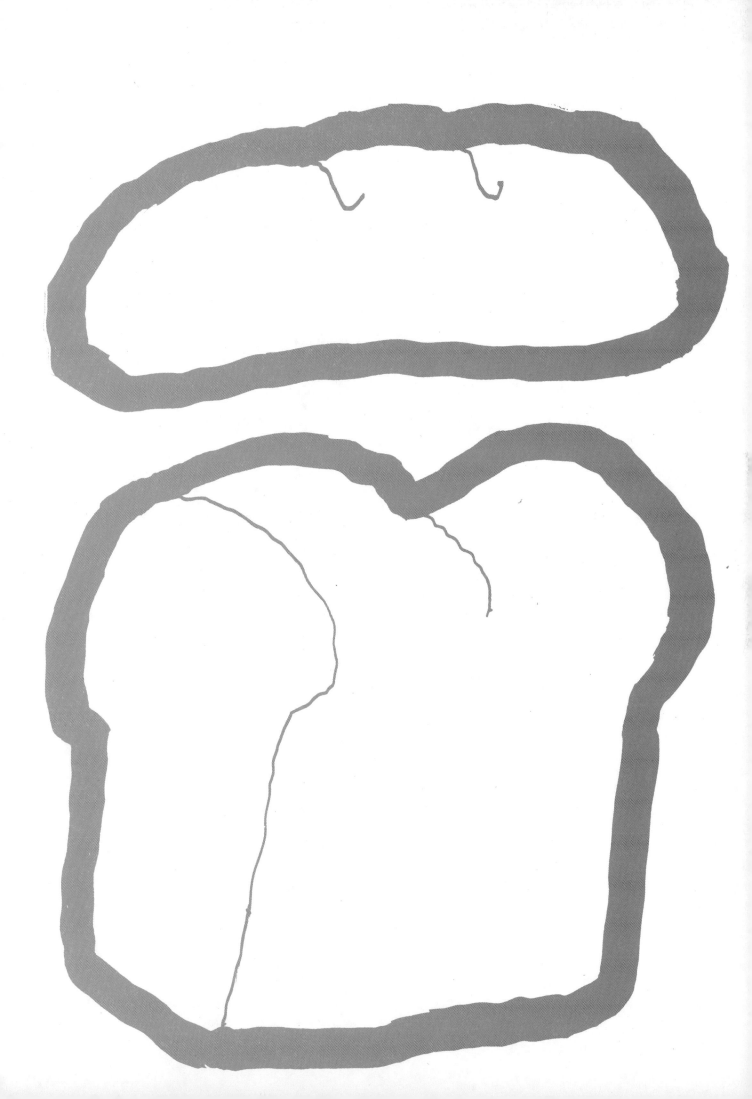

These are lockers

Number them in the right order

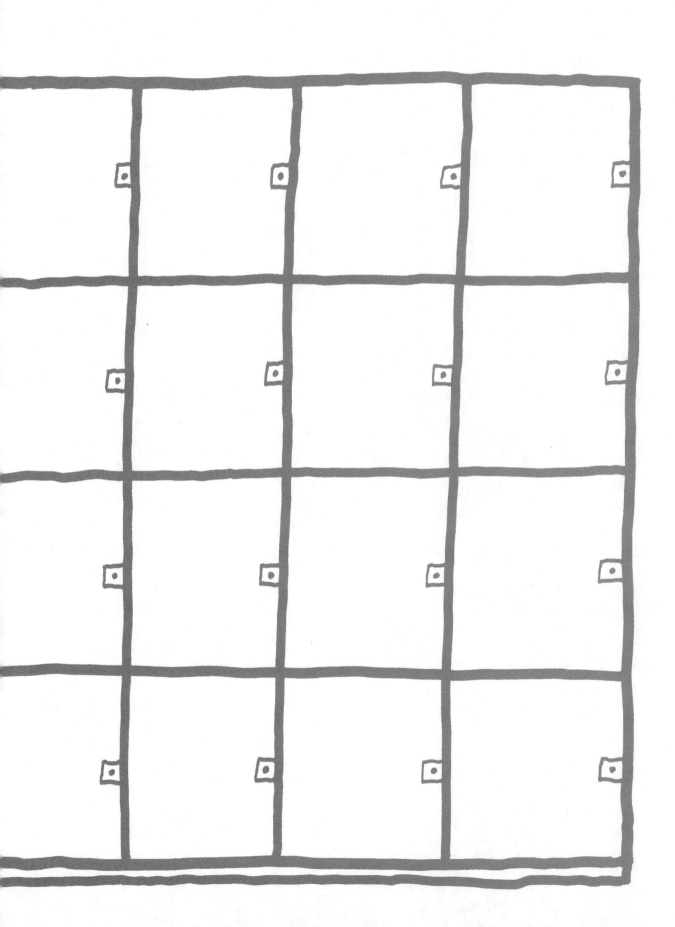

Secret

Draw something secret

Then cut it out and hide it

cut

This is a postcard

Draw and write something that happened to you and cut it out

cut

cut

Back of the postcard

Back of the envelope

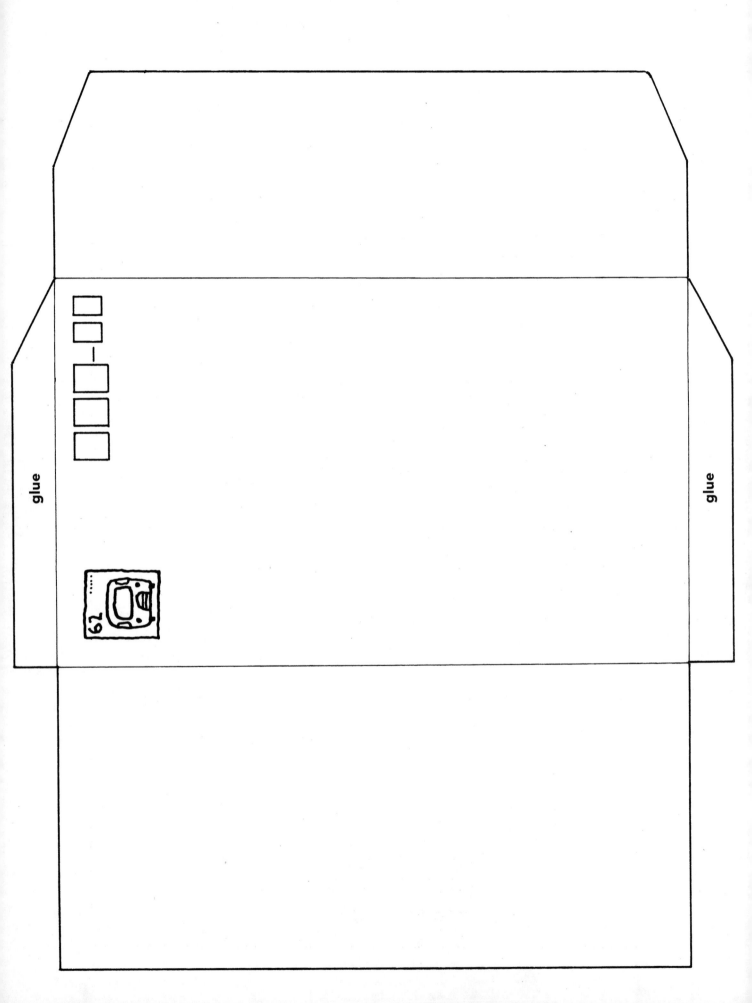

_____

_____

_____

_____

_____

_____

_____

_____

_____

Back of the stationery

Back of the envelope

Write another letter

glue

glue

Back of the stationery

Back of the envelope

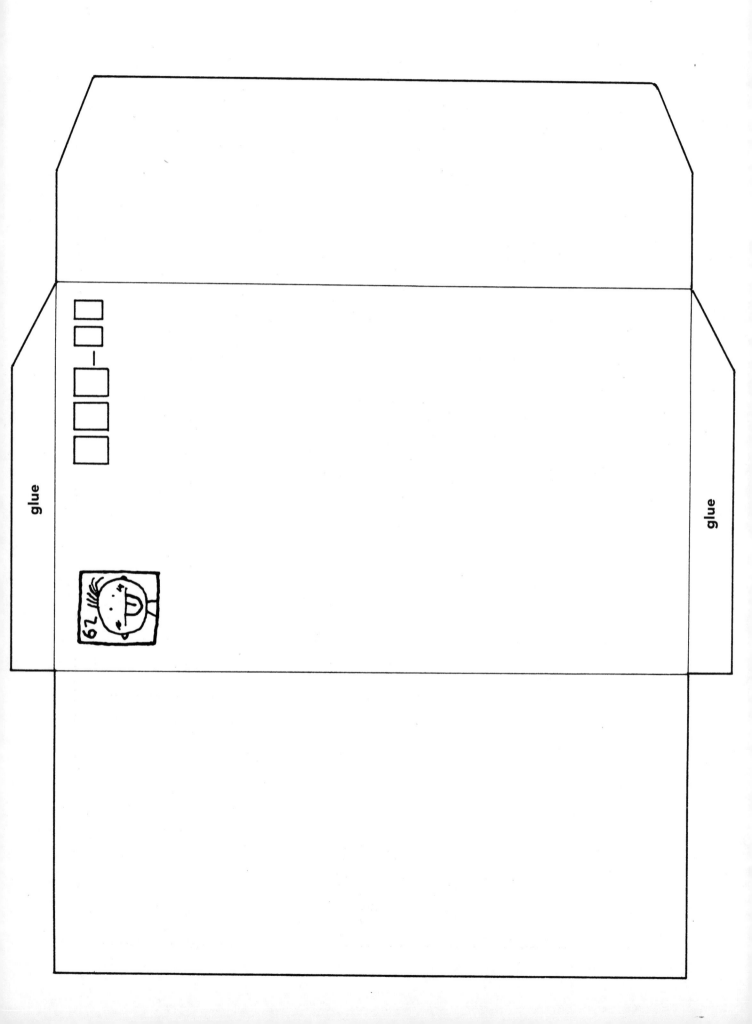

Back of the stationery